WEAKNESS
is NOT SIN

Also by Wendy Ulrich

Forgiving Ourselves:
Getting Back Up When We Let Ourselves Down

WEAKNESS
is NOT SIN

The Liberating

Distinction

That Awakens

Our Strengths

WENDY ULRICH

DESERET
BOOK

SALT LAKE CITY, UTAH

Library of Congress Cataloging-in-Publication Data

Ulrich, Wendy.
  Weakness is not sin : the liberating distinction that awakens our strengths / Wendy L. Ulrich.
    p. cm.
  Includes bibliographical references and index.
  ISBN 978-1-60641-139-1 (paperbound)
  1. Character—Religious aspects—Church of Jesus Christ of Latter-day Saints. 2. Self-actualization (Psychology)—Church of Jesus Christ of Latter-day Saints. 3. Christian life—Mormon authors. I. Title.
  BX8656.U47 2009
  248.4—dc22   2009018672

Printed in the United States of America
R. R. Donnelley, Harrisonburg, VA

10   9   8   7   6

My grace is sufficient for thee:
for my strength is made perfect in weakness.

2 Corinthians 12:9

For my father, Les Woolsey,
and my father-in-law, Richard Ulrich.
We miss you.

CONTENTS

Chapter 1

LEARNING FROM WEAKNESS, LIVING FROM STRENGTH

This book is based on two very simple ideas:

Weakness and sin are very different.

Weakness and strength are not.

Although these ideas are grounded in the scriptures, they run counter to the way we often think. And the way we often think can interfere with our peace, our progress, and our relationship with God.

I never gave much thought to the difference between sin and weakness until recently. I assumed that weakness and sin differed only in degree of seriousness. I heard people pray, "Heavenly Father, forgive us for our sins and weaknesses," and I also lumped the two together without a second thought. Along with most Latter-day Saints, I assumed that sin and weakness were simply different-sized stains on the dirty clothes I wear, different amounts of my indebtedness to the mercy of God.

I also assumed weakness and strength were opposites—that just makes sense, doesn't it? Or does it?

Have you ever noticed that some weaknesses can be seeds of

great spiritual power? Or how often a person's life mission emerges from the strengths and gifts God develops from their weakness? As I have reflected on these possibilities I have realized that weakness and strength are not always opposites, and weaknesses are not always negative. Scriptural teachings seem to confirm this possibility, as when the apostle Paul writes, "When I am weak, then am I strong" (2 Corinthians 12:10).

While some of us are overconfident of our strength and righteousness when in fact we have a lot of work to do, I believe many good Latter-day Saints don't "get" how good they really are. I've come to believe that not understanding the difference between sin and weakness or the relationship between weakness and strength can fuel this chronic feeling of insufficiency. We can find evidence of our insufficiency everywhere—in last week's uninspiring (or nonexistent) family home evening lesson, yesterday's missed deadline, or this morning's impatience with a fellow commuter. We tune out the sacrament meeting speaker who glows about family history because family history is just one item on a long list of our neglected virtues—a list we can't imagine ever fully tackling, a list always standing between us and the Lord. We make New Year's resolutions to chip away at some weakness and then make the same resolutions a year later, and a year later, wondering how long God will put up with us. We berate ourselves for our less-then-stellar Sunday School lesson, our annoyance with our children, our lackluster prayers, our fifteen extra pounds, our irritability with coworkers, our messy garage, our lack of professional development and take it as a given that God's reaction to these "sins and weaknesses" would be disappointment, even anger, for our lack of commitment, charity, obedience, or sacrifice. We contemplate longingly how much better our lives would be if we could just get rid of those pesky weaknesses that undermine our strengths and separate us from God.

We also get stuck on the question, "Do you consider yourself worthy in every way to enter the temple?" We know what the answer to this question is supposed to be, but we wonder how anyone could ever feel worthy in every way to enter a place where "no unclean thing shall be permitted to come" (D&C 109:20). We wonder, "What does it take to be worthy? How far down the list of my shortcomings must I go, how many of my failings must I overcome, to be considered clean? If God cannot look upon sin with the least degree of allowance, what must He think of me? I have so far to go."

We don't just think such thoughts because we lack self-esteem or self-discipline. We may think this way because we mistakenly lump sin and weakness together and assume that guilt and shame are the appropriate response to both.

I have come to believe that my quandary about these things has been based on a mistaken assumption—the mistaken assumption that weakness is sin. As I have carefully considered the Lord's teachings about sin and weakness, a different assumption has taken shape in my mind and heart about how God views these two human conditions. With that changed view has come clarity about how weak and fallen mortals can still be clean, worthy, and welcome in God's presence.

Let me reiterate this alternative premise: sin and weakness are very different. They have different origins and different consequences, call for different remedies, evoke different responses from heaven, reside in different aspects of our being, and produce different effects. Sin can take us to hell. Weakness can take us to heaven.

Sin makes us unworthy to enter God's presence, temple, and kingdom. Sin creates a big problem with eternal consequences. Sin alienates us from ourselves, from the people we sin against, and from our God, who cannot look upon sin with the least degree of allowance. Sin is a choice to follow Satan, the adversary and deceiver.

No matter how strong we become, our spiritual progress and joy—the purposes of mortality—will grind to an absolute halt unless we repent of our sins. As long as we are in a state of sin we can never be worthy to enter God's presence. But through the Atonement of Jesus Christ and subsequent to our repentance, *we can be clean from sin*. Here. Now.

In contrast, our weakness may make us wince at our folly or embarrass our children, but it does not in itself make us unclean. Weakness is in fact a big part of what we came to mortality to experience and something from which we have much to learn. Weakness is inevitable. Weakness may also hurt those we love, cause us significant problems, and call us to regret, apologies, and hard work, but weakness does not have to alienate us from our Father in Heaven. *We will never get rid of all our weakness in this life,* but God's grace can make "weak things become strong"—although not always in the ways we anticipate. His "grace is sufficient for all men that humble themselves before [Him]" (Ether 12:27). Ultimately God's capacity to make weak things become strong is perhaps His most wondrous and distinguishing act of creativity, genius, and love.

I've come to conclude that weakness can actually contribute enormously to our spiritual progress and joy *if* we respond to it with humility and the ability to learn. Great strengths can come out of weakness. Such strengths are grounded in the lessons, perspectives, and virtues we can gain as we turn to God with our limitations, pain, disease, struggle, and affliction. The spiritual gifts, talents, and character virtues worthy of our most concerted effort and energy can emerge from our experience with mortal weakness. Our personal mission includes the callings, causes, and relationships through which we contribute these strengths to the world.

This is not to suggest, however, that God wants us to be constantly preoccupied with our weakness. Of course we want to improve, but in that process it is vital we not lose sight of our strengths—our gifts, our goodness, our talents, our virtues. Although weakness can be our great tutor and the seedbed of our greatest learning, ultimately, I believe, *we are here to magnify our strengths, our callings, and our gifts*—not to magnify our brokenness.

SOME DEFINITIONS

In order to clarify the relationship between weakness, sin, and strength, some definitions are in order. I am using these words as they seem to be most consistently (although not uniformly) used in the scriptures:

Weakness is inherent in the mortal body—which is fashioned from the elements of the earth, shaped by circumstances and experience, and subject to temptation, sickness, injury, fatigue, and death. Out of this general state of human *weakness* we experience specific *weaknesses* such as variations in mental or physical well-being, vulnerability to desires and appetites, predispositions to various physical and emotional states, or differing levels of talents or abilities. All these varying attributes come with the territory of having a mortal body.

Sin is a state of rebellion against God. It almost always involves believing Satan over God about what is real, what is useful, or what will make us happy. It often entails self-centeredness, self-deception, and selfishness. Satan tempts us to rebel against God by playing to our weaknesses to entice us to sin. Our specific *sins* are the behaviors, thoughts, and attitudes that enact our choice to believe Satan over God about what is true, right, or helpful. Sin stops our progress in spiritual things and alienates us from the Spirit. Only by repenting of our sins—changing our minds, hearts, and behavior—can we access the Atonement of Christ and qualify for forgiveness. This process returns us to a state of cleanliness before God.

Strength in its highest sense is what makes us more like God. While we often think of strength as having to do with our abilities and talents, the strength that interests God has to do with our character—our moral choices, our spiritual gifts, and our righteous desires. When we repent of our sins and are humble about both our weak human condition and our specific weaknesses, God can help us turn the weakness of being mortal to the strength of blessing others and becoming more like Him. Some of our specific *strengths* apparently came with us from the premortal experience; others are ours by blessing from the Lord as part of our mortal stewardship; still others we develop here out of weakness through God's grace.

HOW THESE CONCEPTS RELATE

While later chapters will elaborate on these distinctions, the following model gives a preliminary picture of the relationships between sin, weakness, and strength. Diagram 1 begins with the Fall. We all come into life in a state of weakness. Weakness is inherent in the divine gift of the mortal body, but weakness itself is *morally* neutral.

As the diagram shows, sometimes we respond to our weakness by believing Satan, which generally involves some form of self-deception. We may also become preoccupied with the opinions of others, feeling pride, shame, fear, anger, or simply indifference to the things of God. These emotional states often push us toward sin, which makes us unclean before God.

The only way out of sin is through repentance, including godly sorrow and trust in the Atonement. When we repent, God promises forgiveness, which returns us to a state of cleanliness before Him.

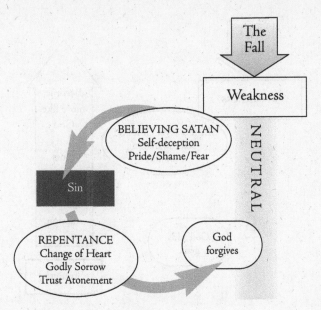

Diagram 1: How Weakness Can Lead to Sin

Diagram 2, which follows, shows us entering the Fall in a state of weakness but responding to our weakness by believing Christ's description instead of Satan's about what is real, useful, and happiness-producing. Believing Christ's description promotes self-awareness and true humility so that we are meek, teachable, non-defensive, willing to learn, and submissive to the Lord. We acknowledge our weaknesses and work to learn and grow. We are patient with ourselves and others.

Through humility we access God's grace, His enabling power to do what we cannot do on our own. When we are humble, God can use our weaknesses to strengthen us. He turns weakness to strength in a variety of ways, only some of which include getting better at things at which we are currently bad.

Even more important than specific improvement in our areas of weakness are such strengths as compassion, faith, courage, creativity, and other spiritual gifts we can acquire as we respond in humility to

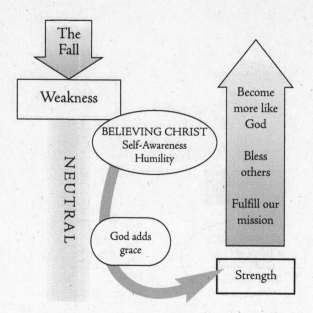

Diagram 2: How Weakness Can Lead to Strength

our weakness. Through such strengths we can bless other people, fulfill our personal mission, and become more like our Father.

Diagram 3 combines the preceding diagrams into one, highlighting the decision we must make about how we will respond to our weakness—either with humility and faith that lead us toward strength, or with pride and self-deception that lead us toward sin. Choosing humility does not mean we will eliminate all our weaknesses, however. Even if we repent from a sin, we will still have weaknesses. Weakness is an inevitable part of the human condition and will never be fully eliminated in this life. We all sin as well, but sin can be eliminated through repentance and reliance on the Atonement. Sin is a choice we can make—or unmake, thanks to Christ's Atonement. Sin is a choice. Weakness is a state.

An example may help clarify the process of responding to our weakness.

Jeremy has a predisposition to serious depression. This mortal weakness may have been inherited from his parents, or may have been learned through some difficult childhood experiences, or both. When Jeremy is overstressed for too long he is especially vulnerable to becoming seriously depressed, sometimes for months at a time.

Serious depression, like any physical or mental illness, is a weakness, not a sin. Depression often includes low energy, low self-esteem, lack of pleasure in former interests, irrational guilt, irritability, difficulty feeling positive feelings (including feeling the Spirit), and suicidal thinking. Satan can use this weakness to undermine Jeremy, tempting him to give up on himself, to withdraw from God and other people, even to take his own life. Jeremy combats some of these temptations but gives in to others (believing Satan).

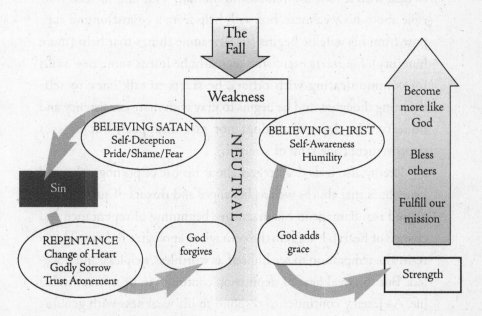

Diagram 3: Weakness, Sin, and Strength

He gets angry at his wife, stops praying, and turns to Internet pornography to try to feel better (sin). These sinful responses make Jeremy feel worse, but he resists the idea of getting professional help for his depression because he worries what others will think (pride/shame/fear). He avoids sharing his real feelings with his wife except when he is totally desperate, and then he tells her in anger that he sees no point to life and wishes his were over, terrifying her. Satan tries to use these feelings of worthlessness and despair to further undermine Jeremy's trust in God's love and compassion. Even in his depressed state, Jeremy knows anger and pornography are alienating him from the Spirit and those he loves, and he feels terrible for violating his own moral code (beginning of repentance).

Over time, Jeremy begins to realize that his depression (a weakness) is creating serious problems in his life and that he needs help to deal with it (self-awareness and humility). At first he feels horrible about his weakness, but with help from a counselor and support from his wife he begins to learn some things that help (more humility). He starts exercising regularly, he learns some new skills for communicating with others, he starts to talk back to self-defeating thoughts, and he begins to pray with more consistency and honesty. His depression does not just disappear, but he sees improvement (one kind of strength).

Jeremy also feels deep regret about his use of pornography, and he realizes that this as well as his anger and threats of suicide have caused real damage in his marriage (beginning of repentance and change of heart). He gains the courage to apologize to his wife and resist the temptation to see himself as worthless, helpless, and hopeless. But the weakness of depression continues to be a factor in his life. As Jeremy continues to respond to his weakness with genuine humility he is less susceptible to the temptation to give up, get angry, hate himself, look at pornography, or act on his suicidal impulses.

He feels God's grace giving him strength beyond his own to remain humble and teachable, even though he still wrestles with his weakness.

Although Jeremy's depression is not eliminated from his life, as he realizes that depression is a weakness and not a punishment or a sin, his trust in God deepens. He and his wife feel closer as they become more honest with each other and as he realizes how much she truly cares for him. When the depression returns, he has more tools for coping with it, and he gets better at resisting temptation and enduring with courage. Because of his own struggles, he feels more empathy with a coworker whose son has a drug problem, and he helps the coworker find an affordable treatment program for his son. Jeremy tries to be more patient with the weaknesses of others (developing and using strengths of compassion, love, courage, and faith). He puts as much energy as he can into loving his family, serving in his calling, and developing and contributing his considerable talents and gifts (focusing on strengths, not weaknesses).

Like Jeremy, we can—at the same time—be trying to determine what in our life is a sin calling for repentance and change, and what is a weakness requiring humility and patient learning. We can also identify, develop, and contribute to the world from our strengths, putting as much energy as we can into this aspect of our personal mission. All are essential to the process of spiritual growth we engage in here.

This book explores several aspects of this process. Chapter 2 discusses the distinction between sin and weakness in more detail. Chapter 3 elaborates on how we can avoid self-deception and gain a better understanding of whether we are dealing with sin or weakness. Chapter 4 examines how repentance (the appropriate response to sin) and humility (the appropriate response to weakness) both resemble each other and differ in important ways. Chapter 5 elaborates on the distinction between shame (and other emotional states that draw us toward sin) and godly sorrow, explaining how godly sorrow but not shame facilitates the repentance process. Chapter 6 delineates several ways grace can operate to turn weakness to strength. Chapter 7 helps us identify our specific strengths, and Chapter 8 reminds us that true strength is always in Christ. The implications of this process become more real as we see how they play out in real life. To illustrate some of these implications, let's consider two stories. The first is about distinguishing sin from weakness. The second is about turning weakness to strength.

A STORY ABOUT SIN AND WEAKNESS

This story comes from the life of a dear friend I'll call Katherine. Katherine married late in life a wonderful man we'll call Dean, a gentle and gifted artist. They were deeply in love and found great delight in each other's company. But Katherine began to notice that Dean was often "forgetful." Experiences Katherine had shared, information she had passed along, even decisions they had made seemed to slip his mind. She soon figured out that this was not some form of early dementia; Dean just wasn't paying attention. He often appeared to be engaged in the conversation when his mind and heart were simply elsewhere, wrapped up in his next artistic project or simply retreating into his long-held private space.

Katherine was confused and increasingly hurt by Dean's lagging concentration. She felt ignored, even rejected, and took her complaint to the Lord. She also talked with Dean to try to figure out what was going on. She thought about his personality, his background, and his otherwise caring heart. The Spirit gradually communicated to her that Dean was in good standing with God and that his inattentiveness to her was not a sin but rather a personal weakness leading to a relationship problem for the two of them to work out together.

Nothing about the way this message was communicated to Katherine felt chastising or uncaring. Instead she felt respected. She was an adult whom God trusted to work out a problem with another adult. Dean's behavior was bothering Katherine, and Katherine's hurt feelings were important to the Lord—but Dean's behavior was not a sin that interfered with his worthiness before God. Even though Dean's actions hurt Katherine and weakened their loving bond, God didn't offer to chastise Dean or pity Katherine. Instead she and Dean continued to work on the problem together through gentle confrontation, careful listening, thoughtful problem solving, and extended effort. They came to a better understanding of each other's needs and personalities. They experimented with ways to improve. Their mutual appreciation and respect grew, along with both greater self-reliance and sweeter interdependence. Their commitment, empathy, and closeness gradually increased. And Katherine began to imagine that a whole host of her own weaknesses and imperfections might also be something God could hold lightly and without ascribing them to sin.

But wait—isn't it selfish and prideful to ignore your wife? Or wasn't it wrong of Katherine to take offense and not just forgive? Aren't such behaviors sinful? Sometimes. And this is where we need the tutoring of the Holy Ghost, the wisdom of the scriptures, a lot of experience, and sometimes the counsel of wise leaders or friends to help us purify our hearts and heal our blindness so we can combat our self-deceptive tendencies and see ourselves and others accurately. There *are* sins we need to repent of, and sometimes they look on the outside very much like weaknesses we need to be humble about. But there are also weaknesses we need to accept with more patience and goodwill rather than berating ourselves or others for them. God, other people, and the school of experience can help us learn the difference.

My hope in this book is to help clarify the important distinction between sin and weakness—to help us define sin, complete the steps of repentance, and qualify for forgiveness, or to help us identify our weaknesses, live skillfully in a state of genuine and deepening humility, and receive God's saving grace. Calling sin weakness can lead to failure to repent, a failure that is fatal to our souls. But calling weakness sin can also have devastating consequences: hopelessness, helplessness, undermined growth and learning, and compromised faith in Jesus Christ, our Savior.

A STORY ABOUT WEAKNESS AND STRENGTH

This book also asserts that as crucial as it is to identify and turn away from our sins, preoccupation with our weaknesses is not really God's desire for us. Mortal weakness is inevitable, instructive, and potentially of great worth as we rely on the Lord, but we are not here to fuss dejectedly and interminably over our weaknesses. We are here to contribute to the world, our families, and the kingdom of God from our strengths. While that is a very small part of diagram 3, I believe God intends it to be a very large part of our lives.

So on to my second story, this time a personal one. I served a mission at the age of twenty-one to France and Belgium. As most missionaries do, I left for my field of labor with high hopes, basking in the expectations of my friends and family. I appeared to have the talent, skills, gospel understanding, and testimony to reach, teach, and bring people to Christ. I had a good background in the French language, a solid understanding of the scriptures, and training as a teacher, and I was the third generation of sister missionaries in my family.

Along with these strengths and advantages I also had some serious weaknesses. I was deeply concerned about my marriage prospects, I lacked discipline and stamina, and I had deep-seated fears of failure and of people, as well as a poor immune system and a predisposition to depression. As a result, I was sick almost constantly, depressed often, not very effective or efficient as a missionary and went home a month early with not-yet-diagnosed mononucleosis that I was sure was simply the ultimate marker of my laziness, lack of commitment, and spiritual failure. Even after being properly diagnosed I assumed my illness was somehow self-induced and self-indulgent. For years I could not go to a missionary farewell or homecoming without stabbing emotional regret and deep shame about my "failure" as a missionary. It appeared for all the world that my weaknesses mattered a lot more than my strengths in determining the effectiveness (or lack thereof) of my mission. But I didn't just feel weak—I felt I was sinful and disappointing to the Lord. My first mission was not really about developing strengths; it was about exposing me to my weaknesses. This was very humbling but—as I learned much later—valuable to my future growth.

Fast-forward thirty years: My husband is called as a mission president to Montreal, Canada, and I am called to serve with him. On receiving my call to return to full-time missionary service, I was at first deeply concerned about my worthiness and capacity to serve given my first missionary "failure." I felt like a hypocrite as I imagined having to teach others about how to be a good missionary. But then I thought, "This time will be different. I have learned the skills of discipline and sacrifice. I can get it right this time. I will get up promptly every morning, read the scriptures for an hour, study with my husband, practice French just like the missionaries, contact everyone I meet, work with the missionaries daily, and never fail my duty. This time I can do it. This time my weaknesses will not undermine me. This time I will succeed."

"This time" didn't last a week. I simply hadn't realized that the expectations for a mission president's wife, at least where we served, are not nearly as predictable or clear-cut as they are for missionaries at large. Despite my commitment and desire, living every mission rule precisely didn't always make sense and was not generally even feasible. But not doing so made me feel like a hypocrite. I could see Missionary Failure #2 looming.

My returned-missionary daughter reminded me, "A teacher at school is not a hypocrite just because she doesn't do all the homework she assigns to students. The teacher's growth will occur differently from the students' growth, and she has a different role to fulfill." Hmmm. Maybe the fact that my Church-provided home included a television set—something missionaries aren't supposed to watch—should have been my first clue the rules might be a little different for me. But how could I know when I was being obedient in principle versus when I was just making excuses for not following every rule in practice? Was I sinning, or weak? I wasn't sure.

As I wrestled with how to prioritize and order my day, I got the distinct spiritual impression, "If you have to choose between reading the scriptures and exercising, exercise." Seldom does spiritual guidance come to me in such distinct and precise terms. I wondered if I could trust such a counterintuitive message. On the other hand, I wasn't too worried about self-indulgent self-deception precisely because I hate to exercise and I generally love reading the scriptures! I discussed my impressions with my husband. We know each other well and are familiar with each other's strengths, weaknesses, and needs. He agreed I should make exercise a priority, and he offered to walk with me.

I soon found myself immersed in the scriptures often and deeply as a natural part of my calling, even though on some days I studied for many hours and other days hardly at all—quite unlike the consistent schedule I had followed as a younger missionary. I also realized that I had spent a lifetime studying the scriptures deeply and that I could draw on that well when time was short. But making time to exercise with any consistency would simply not have happened without major effort to obey the spiritual prompting I received—especially in Montreal weather. Unexpectedly, my (nearly) daily walks with my husband became our planning time, our marriage counseling, our primary emotional connection, and the impetus for our most creative and spiritual insights about our assigned labor. And when the weather was really awful, I learned I could walk on our treadmill and read my scriptures at the same time.

Amazingly, despite extreme temperatures, consistent sleep deprivation, a mediocre immune system, and relentless stress, I was not sick one day of our mission. In fact, I'm sure it was the only three-year time period in my life without a single cold or illness. By obeying a counterintuitive impression from the Spirit, I saw God make my weak immune system, my marriage, and my spiritual life become strong in ways I could not have anticipated.

There were also other ways my early weaknesses as a missionary became strengths for me. Because of that early experience I had great empathy with missionaries who were sick, who had to go home early, or who struggled with depression, discouragement, or lack of skill. I could relate to and understand many of the challenges they faced. My weaknesses helped me better understand other people who shared them, thus increasing my compassion and usefulness. As I pondered and prayed about my weaknesses (like fear of contacting strangers or lack of skill in inviting people to have the missionary lessons) I gained insights that could help not only me but others. Some of my most helpful ideas about how to do missionary work evolved as I dissected my specific worries and skill deficits and got curious about how to improve or work around them.

My weaknesses as a missionary didn't really change—I never excelled at contacting or inviting—but members and missionaries alike knew I had the same fears and failings they did. They couldn't write me off as someone unlike them for whom missionary work came naturally. We were in the process of learning together. After returning home I was asked to join an advisory committee for missionary mental health issues, where my experience with weakness gives me empathy and perspective from which to develop materials that can strengthen others. It didn't all happen when I was twenty-one, but over the course of a lifetime of service, God made much of that early weakness, helping it become a strength that allowed me to bless others.

But I'm getting ahead of myself. Back in Montreal on our mission, I was still acutely aware of my many *current* weaknesses and failings as a missionary and as a mission leader. I won't bore you with the details of my inadequacies and downright stupidities, but there were many. I saw glaring holes in my personality, major deficits in my skills and attitude, unhealed emotional wounds that affected my judgment, and flaws and failings that left me feeling like a hypocrite as I tried to teach and lead among missionaries, members, and investigators. As I struggled with my feelings of guilt and frustration the Spirit came through with a second clear and direct message: "I did not call you here so you could eliminate your weaknesses. I called you to serve from your strengths."

This was an amazing idea for me. I began to see that my preoccupation with my weaknesses was more about pride than righteous desire and that whining about my inadequacy was more annoying than sanctifying. I wasn't just a bundle of weaknesses. I also had strengths. In fact, awareness of my inadequacy was one of them. And while it was good for me to keep trying at things I didn't do well, my energy was best spent contributing from my talents and gifts, not just slaving away at my weaknesses. I didn't have perfect French, but I had a good ear for language and was the first mission president's wife in years to come with a background in it. I was a trained and experienced psychologist. I had years of experience in the scriptures and in teaching. And I had been blessed with a deep love for the elders and sisters. I began to put my energy into developing talks and training material, counseling with troubled missionaries, and participating in mission affairs. I went out of my way to respond to requests to accompany missionaries in teaching, to speak at member events, and to open our home to investigators. These things were not exactly easy (especially in another language), but they were closer to my strike zone. I realized I was most effective when I could contribute from my relative strengths, gifts, and passions, rather than spending too much time fighting against my weaknesses.

I've seen others serve both kinds of missions as well—the kind where God probes, exposes, and calls upon us to work with and contribute from our weaknesses without giving up in shame or frustration, and the kind where He asks us to learn genuine humility even while owning and developing our gifts and strengths. He asks for both our poverty and our riches. Each is its own kind of consecration.

Our personal mission lies in both learning from our weakness and contributing to others from our strength. Developing and contributing our strengths, virtues, aspirations, and gifts is vital to truly living in the fullest and most spiritual sense of that word. At the same time, humility keeps us from basing our self-worth on what we can do. Who we are—our character virtues and spiritual gifts, regardless of our particular skills or talents—is not only enough but all that really matters in terms of God's purposes for us.

As we repent of our sins, respond with humility to our weakness, and develop and contribute our strengths, God's grace is sufficient to save and exalt even the weakest among us.

Even me. Even you.

Chapter 2

DISTINGUISHING SIN
FROM WEAKNESS

Exactly what is sin, what is weakness, how are they different, and why does it matter? Understanding these terms is not just a matter of semantics. It is a matter of understanding God's plan for us, His promises to us, and His relationship with us. A better understanding of the difference between weakness and sin (diagram 1, chapter 1) can help us find both the pathway toward the loving face of God and joy in our redemption.

Most of us are fairly clear about what sin includes and how it differs from weakness when we really stop and think about it, but sometimes we don't stop and think, and then we get offtrack. So let's do a brief review that will help us distinguish sin from weakness.

SINFUL BY CHOICE

In a phrase, sin is rebellion against the light of God. On a practical level, we sin when we know right from wrong and choose to do wrong. We can learn right from wrong from other people or from the promptings of our conscience—we don't have to know God to be guilty of wrongdoing. But the more we know God and His commandments, the more we stand to gain the blessings associated with being in a relationship with Him and the more we become guilty of sin when we turn our backs on Him.

We have to know better to be accountable for sin. Children and people who have not known God's will are not accountable for sin in the same way as those who know better. As Moroni 8:8, 11 explains, "Little children are whole, for they are not capable of committing sin" and so they "need no repentance, neither baptism." For this reason "all little children are alive in Christ, and also all they that are without the law" (v. 22). Jesus also taught:

"And that servant, which knew his lord's will, and prepared not himself, neither did according to his will, shall be beaten with many stripes. But he that knew not, and did commit things worthy of stripes, shall be beaten with few stripes. For unto whomsoever much is given, of him shall be much required: and to whom men have committed much, of him they will ask the more" (Luke 12:47–48).

We can also sin by failing to do right: "Therefore to him that knoweth to do good, and doeth it not, to him it is sin" (James 4:17).

Elder Orson F. Whitney of the Quorum of the Twelve Apostles, as quoted in the *Encyclopedia of Mormonism*, expounds: "Sin is the transgression of divine law, as made known through the conscience or by revelation. A man sins when he violates his conscience, going contrary to light and knowledge—not the light and knowledge that has come to his neighbor but that which has come to himself. He sins when he does the opposite of what he knows to be right. Up to that point he only blunders. One may suffer painful consequences for only blundering, but he cannot commit sin unless he knows better."[1]

Even if we do not know God, His basic laws are found among every people, and the Spirit of Christ informs our conscience and understanding of right and wrong. When we choose to ignore what we know is right, we are guilty of sin. When we know God and have covenanted to obey Him, not only do we violate our own conscience when we sin but we also turn away from God and our covenant relationship with Him.

Depending on what we have been taught or felt in our hearts, we may be accountable at different levels for sin. The scriptures teach that sin includes violating the Ten Commandments: murder, adultery, lying, stealing, coveting, dishonoring the Sabbath, dishonoring parents, taking the name of the Lord in vain, or worshiping something or someone other than God. For members of the Church who have been so taught, sin also includes actions or beliefs that would keep us out of the temple or that would jeopardize our membership in the Church. We sin when we ignore our duty in the Church, when we consistently fail to pray, or when we withhold our substance from the poor. There are many ways to sin, but they all boil down to a willful turning away from the light we have. Even if the adversary succeeds in deceiving us, we are guilty of sin as we participate in our own deception, trusting our own reasoning or desires over our baptismal or temple covenants.

Satan is the author of sin in this world. He stirs up people "to do iniquity" (D&C 10:29), tries "to deceive [us]" (50:3), and seeks "to turn [our] hearts away from the truth" (78:10). He is "the father of all lies" (Moses 4:4). But Satan cannot make us sin. Sin is resident in our agency, our choices. It thus reflects our desires and our loyalty. Sin is a choice to believe Satan over God about what will make us happy, what will produce a certain result, or what will do the most good in the long run. No one else can force us to sin, even if they can overpower us and force us to do something terrible, because sin is not just what we do; it is what we desire, what we love, and what we choose. Sin leads us away from heaven and toward hell. Sin is the enemy of our soul.

WEAK BY DESIGN

In contrast, weakness is resident in the nature of mortality and the experience of being human. Nephi, worried about errors in his record, reminds himself that errors were also made by other writers, adding, "not that I would excuse myself because of other men, but because of the weakness which is in me, according to the flesh, I would excuse myself" (1 Nephi 19:6). Weakness is inherent in human flesh; it comes with the territory of having a body and being mortal.

We learn in Ether 12:27 that God gives us weakness in order to help accomplish His purposes: "And if men come unto me I will show unto them their weakness. I give unto men weakness that they may be humble; and my grace is sufficient for all men that humble themselves before me; for if they humble themselves before me, and have faith in me, then will I make weak things become strong unto them."

If for no other reason, it is crucial to distinguish sin from weakness because Satan is the author of sin, while weakness is part of God's plan. While sin and weakness may look alike to others (just as lust and love may look alike in some ways, or pride and confidence, or stubbornness and integrity), this surface similarity can be misleading. Sin and weakness are very different. Satan will attempt to exploit our weakness, tempting us to use it as an excuse to give in to sin, and we may contribute to our weakness by putting ourselves in compromising situations, ignoring counsel, neglecting our soul's education, or failing to take care of our bodies. For all of these things we may suffer severe consequences. Nevertheless, the weakness of being mortal (limited, vulnerable, and inadequate) is not in itself sin. We are all weak, by virtue of being human.

Specific weaknesses might include the following:

+ Physical disease such as heart disease, diabetes, cancer, malaria, or a simple sore throat

+ Emotional illnesses such as depression, attention deficits, bipolar disorder, anxiety, or narcissism

+ Susceptibility to temptations such as lust, greed, pride, envy, and laziness (giving in to these temptations may be sinful, but being tempted is not)

+ Predispositions we are born with, including everything from addiction, same-gender attraction, and obesity to intelligence, extraversion, and musical aptitude (again, weakness is morally neutral, and even seeming strengths can create problems, depending on how we use them)

+ Suffering that comes with having been traumatized, abandoned, neglected, or betrayed

+ Susceptibility to loss and grief because of our own impending death or the death of those we love (even though death itself is often a great blessing)

+ Certain emotions such as sadness, grief, shame, anger, impatience, worry, jealousy, and guilt, as well as pleasure, excitement, relaxation, and satisfaction (which can also become hedonism, anxiety, laziness, and addiction if misdirected)

+ Deficits we have experienced because of our upbringing or culture

+ Limitations on our time, energy, experience, skills, knowledge, and emotional capacity, as well as limitations on how much we know

This is an important list to contemplate. Because we are weak we are slow, limited, broken, ignorant, and mediocre. Even our positive emotions and predispositions to talent or intelligence are morally neutral and can lead to either strength or sin depending on how we use them. We are expected to seek education, work to improve, avoid tempting situations, care for our bodies and spirits, learn from mistakes, keep trying, and get help. All these things will help us manage our specific weaknesses more successfully, but we will still be mortal and therefore weak. And weakness is our gift from a loving Father.

	SIN	WEAKNESS
Definition	Willful rebellion against God	Human limitations and vulnerabilities
Part of whose plan?	Satan's	God's
Resident in . . .	Human agency	The mortal body

Diagram 4: Definitions of Sin and Weakness

THE REMEDY FOR SIN

Not only do sin and weakness differ but the courses of action required for each differ. The scriptures and the prophets make clear what our course of action should be if we are guilty of sin: repent! To repent is to change our mind, our heart, and ultimately our behavior. Repentance is not just about changing, however; it is recognition that we have been wrong and that we have been believing Satan over God.

We may have learned some of the steps of repentance in Primary, but we deepen our understanding of it as adults. We know we must first *recognize* that we have sinned and are in a state of rebellion against God. We will feel the deep *regret* or godly sorry that accompanies awareness of the damage we have done and the disloyalty we have demonstrated. We will *confess* to those we have injured, apologize and ask forgiveness, and make *restitution* in whatever way possible. We will pay the penalty or *accept the consequences* associated with our sin, recognizing that we have caused harm and have incurred a debt. We will *pray*, pleading with God for forgiveness in deep humility. And we will *forsake the sin* and never do it again. In fact, with genuine repentance sin becomes abhorrent to us—we deeply understand that it violates God's teachings, and we never want to find ourselves in a situation of this kind of enmity with God again. Repentance is not just regret and not just refraining from our old ways. Repentance is a change of mind and heart as well as behavior.

Alma the Younger, after he "beheld an angel of the Lord" (Mosiah 27:18), repents sufficiently while in a sort of comatose state to "behold the marvelous light of God" (v. 29). He had been in a state of terrible sin, seeking to destroy the Church of God, and yet he reports that God has redeemed him even before his repentance has led him to change his behavior. Alma changes his mind and his heart, "wading through much tribulation, repenting nigh unto death" without moving a muscle (v. 28). Afterwards he is no longer tempted by his sin—he doesn't go around thinking, "I sure would like to destroy somebody's soul today, but I guess I'd better not." He does not have to fight within himself, resist, or struggle to restrain himself from destroying the Church. Once he fully understands that he had been fighting against God he is horrified at his sin, deeply regrets it, and never repeats it. He spends the rest of his life living out of that repentance, that change of mind and heart, and making restitution for his sin. As we know from experience, not all sins are as readily forsaken, but Alma provides a model or prototype of repentance.

THE OUTCOME OF REPENTANCE

Once we truly repent, God promises to forgive us. He says: "Behold, he who has repented of his sins, the same is forgiven, and I, the Lord, remember them no more. By this ye may know if a man repenteth of his sins—behold, he will confess them and forsake them" (D&C 58:42–43). To repent is to change our mind, turn our heart and will to God, and renounce sin (see Bible Dictionary, "Repentance").[2] When we *truly and sincerely* repent, God forgives. That's it. End of story. Done. Our debt is transferred to the Savior, our soul is no longer at enmity with God, Satan's grasp on us is released, and we are clean. This is the miracle made possible through the Atonement of Jesus Christ. It would be worth a whole library of books to simply contemplate the wonder of this transcendent gift. When we repent, God forgives.

So if God forgives, why do people still have to go to prison if they are sorry for what they did wrong? Why might individuals still be excommunicated or disfellowshipped even if they feel bad for their error? Why might we be restricted as to Church positions we can hold even after we have repented? Why might certain opportunities, perhaps even promised in our patriarchal blessing, be withheld?

First, if we are truly repentant, we *want* to pay whatever small price we can pay to show our renewed commitment to God's laws. We want to make it a little easier for those we have injured to forgive us by participating in the process of justice and joining in some of the suffering we have inflicted. We want to help make restitution by being a willing object lesson in teaching others about the consequences of sin. And we want to demonstrate our true sorrow. We may not enjoy it, and God and the courts may not always require it, but we are willing to pay whatever we can against the debt we have incurred from those we have injured.

The restrictions we submit to are not just God lowering the boom on us. When God takes away certain opportunities, He is not simply punishing us; He may be protecting us. For example, He may be shielding us from the public scrutiny of visible positions. He may be safeguarding us, keeping us from compounding the damage we have done by seeming to portray that sin is without consequences. He may be helping us combat pride by resisting our errant notion that Church position is a celestial stamp of approval. He may be helping us learn the crucial truth that visible callings are not the evidence of His love or the only pathway to His glory. He may be offering us saving lessons in humility without humiliation. We can still be confident we have a place in His promise: "But as oft as they repented and sought forgiveness, with real intent, they were forgiven" (Moroni 6:8).

Forgiveness is made possible through the Atonement of Jesus Christ. We do not need to wonder or speculate about whether forgiveness will come. God's promise is unequivocal: If we truly repent, He forgives. We don't have to wait for a voice from heaven, a burning in the bosom, a sign, a feeling, reinstatement of our privileges, the end of our prison term, or the forgiveness of others to know that God will forgive us. His promise is sure: If we truly repent—renounce our sin, do all we can to make it right, and return to God—He will forgive.

President Boyd K. Packer reiterates:

"Restoring what you cannot restore, healing the wound you

cannot heal, fixing that which you broke and cannot fix is the very purpose of the atonement of Christ.

"When your desire is firm and you are willing to pay the 'uttermost farthing' (see Matt. 5:25–26), the law of restitution is suspended. Your obligation is transferred to the Lord. He will settle your accounts.

"I repeat, save for the exception of the very few who defect to perdition, there is no habit, no addiction, no rebellion, no transgression, no apostasy, no crime exempted from the promise of complete forgiveness. This is the promise of the atonement of Christ."[3]

Through His wondrous Atonement, the Savior pays the debt we incur through sin, washes us through His blood, and we are clean. Satan has no claim on us, and hell can no longer hold us. We may still have many weaknesses, much to learn, many virtues to acquire, important work to complete, and vital relationships to build. But we are clean. We are still weak: fallen, inadequate, limited, tempted, sick, ignorant, faulty, unskilled, broken, and vulnerable. But we are clean. We don't have to be without flaw or blemish to be freed from sin if we have repented and turned back to God. We are clean. *We are clean.* This is a cause for great joy.

THE REMEDY FOR WEAKNESS

The course of action required in the case of weakness is different in important ways from the course required for sin. The verse in Ether 12:27 quoted previously makes clear what the course of action should be for the weak. They are to "humble themselves before me, and have faith in me." What might the steps of humility and faith in response to weakness include? Are they different from the steps of humility and faith required for repentance?

I think some of the steps of repentance (like recognizing and regretting our sins and trying to make right the harm we have caused) also apply to the process of humbling ourselves about our weakness, but they don't all work quite the same way when we are dealing with weakness. This is especially true for the step about never doing it again.

In our weakness we are in fact very likely to "do it again." We will get better at some things—many things—but probably not all things, and not all of the time. We will need to keep working to keep improving. Temptation will not just disappear from our lives. We will struggle against some habits and patterns for a long time. We will continue to be subject to human illness, emotion, and limitations. Someone else will always be better than we are at specific skills and traits. In mortality we will always be weak, we will always have some of our weaknesses, and we will always need God's grace to respond constructively. But weakness is not sin!

When we *recognize* that our weakness is causing problems for us or others, we may *regret* our behavior, attempt to *reform*, even make *restitution* if possible, but we will *not* necessarily *resolve* never to do that thing again because it is often not that simple. Sometimes (for example, if our weakness has led to a bad judgment call and we come to see the error of our ways) we will not repeat our mistake. With other issues we will spend a lifetime learning to work with our weakness—for example, when dealing with human emotion, susceptibility to physical or mental illness, or limits on our knowledge and skill. With such weaknesses there is a high probability we will be ignorant again, get sick again, be incompetent again, and make mistakes again because that is the nature of weakness. We will again face the temptation to be prideful, uncharitable, faithless, or judgmental, and even though these behaviors and attitudes are sinful, being tempted with them is not. Our predispositions to addiction, anger, same-sex attraction, or rash decision-making will not just disappear at will. Our upbringing, genes, habits, and patterns of perception will continue to influence us. Our ignorance, limited perspective, and superstition will not be conquered overnight. But such weakness is not sin!

In other words, weakness is not just a choice we make (as sin is); weakness means vulnerabilities and limitations we must sometimes learn to live with, even as we try to improve, grow, and learn. In humility we acknowledge that we must be patient with the process of growth, be open to help and support, and be practical about our priorities because we cannot do everything at once. In humility we turn and submit ourselves to God for direction and help, to other people for charity and patience, and to our strengths for compensation. We recognize that we will never overcome all our weakness in this life. Ever. But weakness is not sin!

If we are truly humble, meek, and teachable in the face of our weakness, we don't just give up on family home evening because we had a bad experience last week, or all last year. We don't just forget about family history because we don't know how to do it or it isn't a reasonable priority today. We don't stop trying to improve just because last year's New Year's resolutions didn't make it to February. We keep working on our endless list: the less-than-stellar Sunday School lessons, our impatience with our children, our lackluster prayers, our fifteen extra pounds, our irritability with coworkers, our messy garage, and all our other human weaknesses. And as we do so we are open to learning, willing to prioritize and to be as prayerful, patient, and honest with ourselves and others as we know how to be. And when we are not, we try again, confident in God's love and grace. Because weakness is not sin!

When the risen Christ confronted Paul on the road to Damascus with his sin of persecuting the Church of Christ, like Alma the Younger, Paul immediately repented. He changed his mind, his heart, and ultimately his behavior. But when he was dealing with a weakness he wrote:

"For this thing I besought the Lord thrice, that it might depart from me. And he said unto me, My grace is sufficient for thee: for my strength is made perfect in weakness. . . . Therefore I take pleasure in infirmities, in reproaches, in necessities, in persecutions, in distresses for Christ's sake: for when I am weak, then am I strong" (2 Corinthians 12:8–10).

There is no need for shame about our weakness just because it puts us out of favor with the world. Not only is weakness not sin but God's grace can turn weakness to strength.

AMAZING GRACE

When we are humble in the face of our weakness, God offers us another form of grace—not exactly the same as the forgiveness He offers the repentant but grace "sufficient for all [those] that humble themselves before me . . . and have faith in me" (Ether 12:27). What exactly is this grace?

The Bible Dictionary describes grace as a "divine means of help or strength, given through the bounteous mercy and love of Jesus Christ." Grace provides "strength and assistance to do good works that [we] otherwise would not be able to maintain if left to [our] own means. This grace is an enabling power that allows men and women to lay hold on eternal life and exaltation." We learn further, "Divine grace is needed by every soul in consequence of the fall of Adam and also because of man's weaknesses and shortcomings." Grace is an enabling power that is God's remedy for human weakness. It is a power we qualify for by both faith and personal effort, but our effort is never sufficient without God's all-sufficient hand. As Nephi teaches, "It is by grace that we are saved, [even] after all we can do" (2 Nephi 25:23).[4]

Ether 12:27 tells us that to qualify for God's grace we must have two things: humility and faith in Christ. In David H. Stern's *Complete Jewish Bible*, the word *trust* is consistently used for the word often translated as *faith*.[5] I really like this translation. For many people "faith" has come to simply mean a set of beliefs, but "trust" also implies a relationship. To have real faith is to trust in Christ's love and in God's plan. It implies we act on our belief, choosing connection with God over rebellion. While God cannot save us in our sins, He has the will and the power to save us in our weakness. Trusting in that love and goodness brings great peace.

When we are humble, God also offers to make "weak things

	SIN	WEAKNESS
Definition	Willful rebellion against God	Human limitations and vulnerabilities
Part of whose plan?	Satan's	God's
Resident in . . .	Human agency	The mortal body
Appropriate response	Repentance	Humility and faith
God's response	Forgiveness	Grace
Results in . . .	Cleanliness	Learning and acquisition of virtue
. . . which leads to . . .	Escape from hell	Exaltation

Diagram 5: Summary of Differences between Sin and Weakness

become strong." God can make us strong in many ways (which we will elaborate on in chapter 5). Sometimes we get better at what we used to be lousy at. Sometimes we come to realize that our weakness has a flip side that in other settings or intensities can be strength. Sometimes we learn to compensate for our weakness by developing completely different strengths. But the most important "strength" God gives us is probably something else entirely. As we shall discuss later, what God does with human weakness, if we are humble and trust Him, is to turn it to our exaltation. This is the power and reach of God's amazing grace (see diagram 5).

WHAT IF I CAN'T TELL THE DIFFERENCE?

As diagram 1 (chapter 1) reminds us, getting us to believe Satan and deceive ourselves is Satan's primary tool in turning our weakness to sin. Being clear about the difference between sin and weakness is one key to avoiding self-deception. It is not always easy to tell the difference between sin and weakness. We can think we are dealing with weakness when we are really in a state of sin; this is an extremely dangerous position because then we don't repent and qualify for forgiveness but remain in our sinful state. We can also think we are dealing with a sin we just can't seem to repent of when we are really dealing with a weakness; this is also a dangerous position because we can easily become discouraged, give up on ourselves and God, stop trying, give in to sin, or deny ourselves the joy and peace that are rightfully ours as those who are actually clean before the Lord.

Making this distinction is not easy—in fact, by nature it is one of the things at which we are weak and imperfect. But as with many weaknesses, we get better at making important distinctions between sin and weakness with practice, help from others, and prayerful contemplation. Being aware that sin and weakness are different is the first, but not the only, step in making this distinction. Chapter 3 will help us further elaborate the process of distinguishing sin from weakness and avoiding self-deception.

The crucial point to be made is that the endless list of our weaknesses may frustrate us, but these weaknesses do not make us unclean. Weakness *by itself* does not make us unworthy to associate with the Holy Ghost, receive answers to our prayers, partake of the sacrament, or ask for help. Despite the messages we get from society and ourselves, weakness is not a cause for shame or guilt, only a cause for meekness, learning, and effort. Weakness is a gift from God to help us learn the humility, faith, and charity that will bring us closer to sitting down with Him.

GOOD COMPANY

Even Jesus Christ, who was completely free from sin, dealt with mortal weakness. He was subject to illness (see Alma 7:11–12); temptation (see Hebrews 4:15); emotions (see Isaiah 53:3); "hunger, thirst, and fatigue" (Mosiah 3:7). He learned through suffering (see Hebrews 5:8), and he had to learn and grow over time (see D&C 93:12–13). He needed succor and help (see Luke 22:43), He suffered in response to other people's poor choices and judgments, and He died. Christ joins us fully in the mortal experience. His Atonement is not just for our sin but also includes in its scope our mortal weakness.

Alma records: "And he shall go forth, suffering pains and afflictions and temptations of every kind; and this that the word might be fulfilled which saith he will take upon him the pains and the sicknesses of this people. And he will take upon him death, that he may loose the bands of death which bind his people; and he will take upon him their infirmities, that his bowels may be filled with mercy, according to the flesh, that he may know according to the flesh how to succor his people according to their infirmities" (Alma 7:11–12). An infirmity is a weakness, imperfection, frailty, or failing.

Let me say it one more time: If we have truly repented of our sins, we can be assured of God's forgiveness. We are clean. The endless list of mortal weakness is not a barrier to this amazing gift. We absolutely need to be humble, but we need not be humiliated about having mortal weakness. We have divine companionship as we struggle with our weakness: the Father, whose plan includes it; the Son, whose atonement makes up for it; and the Holy Ghost, who comforts and strengthens us as we rely upon God. Weakness is a divine gift essential to the experience of mortality. And through this weakness, God can do amazing things.

Chapter 3

INCREASING SELF-AWARENESS, AVOIDING SELF-DECEPTION

My name is Wendy, and I'm a sinner. I don't think I've committed a single sin yet this morning, but I've committed my share over a lifetime, and I have no reservations about the likelihood that I will commit more before I die, although I'm certainly not planning on it. I'm very committed to the gospel of Jesus Christ, I love the Lord, I want to be obedient, and I consider it a privilege to know and keep His commandments. But I also know that, like alcoholics who can't trust themselves with alcohol, I can't trust myself to steer clear of sin. When I sin, there is nothing more important than repenting (changing my mind and heart), stopping the sinful behavior, and seeking God's forgiveness and the forgiveness of others. Nothing.

I'm also a weakling. In fact, today and most days my state of weakness is a bigger concern to me than my sins, for one simple reason: at least up to this point I've repented of my sins, but my weakness is ever before me. In fact, my inadequacies, flaws, limitations, and vulnerabilities are virtually limitless. I eat too much sugar, my selfishness is scary, I'm tempted by envy and sloth, I don't like wearing my seatbelt, I try to do too much and then I get irritable and annoying, I don't stretch enough, I'm shy, I haven't made my bed, I get obsessed with what I'm doing and ignore important things, I don't like to answer the phone, I didn't work very hard on my Sunday School lesson this week, I hate gardening . . . the list of my weaknesses goes on and on. I could make an argument for every single one of these items being sinful, but I think most of them are more accurately and helpfully understood as weaknesses.

WATCHING OUR WEAKNESSES

Allen got so overwhelmed with the long "to do" list in the Church that he simply gave up. Even though he had served in responsible Church positions in which he had helped others to repent, when he was tempted with a serious sin he gave in, thinking that he could never fulfill all the requirements of Church membership anyway so he might as well quit now. Not realizing that his weaknesses (emotions, ignorance, limitations on his time and energy, and susceptibility to temptation) were not sins, he succumbed to real sin, seeing it as inevitable. While Allen undoubtedly participated in his own self-deception, his story reminds us that Satan can use our misunderstanding of the difference between sin and weakness against us.

Sin and weakness may both play a role in a given problem. We may need to both repent of the sin and continue to struggle with our human weakness in humility. For example, we may need to repent of the sin of using drugs when we know it is wrong. We will need to change our mind and heart, regret our rebellious choice, make restitution, apologize, and resolve to change. But we may still struggle for a long time against the weakness of the flesh that leads to drug addiction. In that struggle we may need to get professional help, remove ourselves from temptation, learn more about addiction, participate in addiction recovery programs, learn better coping skills, ask friends and family for support, invite priesthood blessings, and so on.

The humility needed in the face of weakness includes being teachable, getting help, learning from our mistakes, restricting our own agency for a time while we learn new skills and habits, and trying again after setbacks. Our weakness may make it difficult to complete all the changes repentance requires, but in humility and faith we keep trying and learning, trusting in the Lord's help, tutoring, and redemptive power.

Parsing out what is sin and what is weakness in a given situation is not always easy. Do I lose my temper because I am weak or because I am sinful? How about overeating? Speeding? Sleeping in? Laughing? Are these sins? Weaknesses? Neither? Both?

King Benjamin in the Book of Mormon reminds his people: "I cannot tell you all the things whereby ye may commit sin; for there are divers ways and means, even so many that I cannot number them. But this much I can tell you, that if ye do not watch yourselves, and your thoughts, and your words, and your deeds, and observe the commandments of God, and continue in the faith of what ye have heard concerning the coming of our Lord, even unto the end of your lives, ye must perish. And now, O man, remember, and perish not" (Mosiah 4:29–30).

Is King Benjamin trying to tell us that everything we think, speak, or do that is not 100 percent perfect is sin? I don't think so. I think he *is* inviting us to do three things: watch ourselves, observe the commandments, and continue in faith in Christ's Atonement.

This chapter is about watching. Not in the sense of "watch out!" but in the sense of literally watching, or *observing*, ourselves, our thoughts, words, and deeds, noticing how we think and speak and act. Trying to better understand ourselves and increase our self-awareness helps us make clearer distinctions between what is sin and what is weakness in us. As we watch ourselves closely we need not become more perfectionistic, obsessive, compulsive, and ashamed. We may become, in fact, more peaceful, joyful, obedient, and grateful.

DISTINGUISHING SIN FROM WEAKNESS

My nephew Brent is a doctor in a residency training program. He is expected to be at the hospital on duty for thirty-six hours straight and then off for twelve hours. He repeats this rotation for the duration of his program. I don't know how people do this, but of course they do. So does that mean that because it is possible to live this way, anyone who doesn't is lazy? That would make me lazy indeed! If so, avoiding "laziness" requires a much bigger sacrifice than I am willing to make. Shall I just accept my "laziness" and not try to do anything about it? Or does God require me to live as my nephew does in order to combat laziness and be anxiously engaged in good things?

It seems sometimes that so much of life is about finding the fine lines between laziness and moderation, between sin and weakness, between the Spirit and our own thoughts, between confidence and pride, between humility and humiliation. But at least it is a start to know that there is in fact a difference and that the difference is worth exploring. Trying to discern the real boundaries and edges of laziness is not easy. We will not always get it right, but we can get closer and closer as we "watch" ourselves and reflect on the results of our choices.

The most common question people ask me about the concepts in this book is, "How can I tell the difference between sin and weakness?" In other words, if I don't want to live like my nephew must live right now, am I being sinful? Weak? Wise? I have found this to be a challenging question, in part because, as we have already seen, the lines between sin, weakness, and strength are to some extent a personal matter. What is sin to you may not be sin to me, depending on what I have been taught, how much I understand, my intentions and desires, my circumstances, the needs of the moment, and the development of my conscience. The Lord talks often of sin in the scriptures, but we must remember the simple fact that He is always speaking to those who are actually reading His words. The same actions may not be counted as sin against those who do not have this light and knowledge.

ACCOUNTABILITY

We might ask, then, "Why would we want to learn about God's expectations if knowing them makes us more accountable for sin? Maybe we are better off staying ignorant!"

God does not say that what we do in ignorance will not harm others or limit our progression—He only says He will not count it as sin against us personally. These same actions are nevertheless hurtful and destructive, even if we are not personally accountable for sin when we do them. The things God commands us not to do will still cause damage whether or not we intend and desire that damage. Conversely, we, our families, and our societies will still be blessed and helped if we observe God's laws whether or not we are aware we are doing so. It is a blessing to learn things that can help us be happier, healthier, and more at peace. I will never be accountable for missing a key shot in an NBA playoff game, because I have never learned the rules or the skills to be able to play. But neither will I ever have the thrill of that victory. God wants to give us all He has, but we must be willing to be accountable for what we do with it. Yes, we will fall less often if we never try to climb, but we will also never get where we want to go. We stand to gain great spiritual power as we learn by our experience good from evil. The Atonement of Christ makes the risks of mortality worth taking. It alone assures that our greater accountability will bless us, not merely leave us stranded with our resulting sins.

I love the classic talk by President Spencer W. Kimball in which he recalls the story of Caleb, a mighty leader in Israel in his day, who is now eighty-five years old. Caleb sees the work still to be done to reclaim the promised land from the unrighteous giants who currently inhabit it. Even at his advanced age he proclaims, "'Give me this mountain.'" President Kimball adds: "This is my feeling for the work at this moment. There are great challenges ahead of us, giant opportunities to be met. I welcome that exciting prospect and feel to say to the Lord, humbly, 'Give me this mountain,' give me these challenges.

"Humbly, I give this pledge to the Lord and to you, my beloved brothers and sisters, fellow workers in this sacred cause of Christ: I will go forward, with faith in the God of Israel, knowing that he will guide and direct us, and lead us, finally, to the accomplishment of his purposes and to our promised land and our promised blessings.

"'And Jesus said unto him, No man having put his hand to the plough, and looking back, is fit for the kingdom of God' (Luke 9:62).

"I will 'wholly follow the Lord my God' to the fullest extent of my energy and my ability.

"Earnestly and fervently I urge that each of you make this same pledge and effort—every priesthood leader, every woman in Israel, each young man, each young woman, every boy and girl."[1]

This is the attitude that fills us with enthusiasm for the opportunity of being accountable to God! In such a frame of mind we understand the blessings that come from being in God's service, and we desire to avoid all the pitfalls we can from being deceived by Satan.

AVOIDING DECEPTION

God promises to help us in our effort to avoid deception about our sins and weaknesses. In fact, He explicitly offers to show us both our sins (see D&C 66:3) and our weaknesses (see Jacob 4:7). In my experience, He expects us to examine our hearts, study the scriptures, counsel with others, and ponder our situation in addition to asking His help with this important distinction.

If we are doing something that is damaging to someone else, that violates our covenants, or that we are hiding from our leaders, we don't really need a personal revelation to guess we are making sinful choices.

By the same token, we may deeply regret something, feel responsible (even have caused harm), wish more than anything that we could go back and undo it, and still be dealing with a human weakness rather than a sin.

For example, in the book *Forgiving Ourselves: Getting Back Up When We Let Ourselves Down*, I tell a story about an incident that caused me deep regret, embarrassment, and pain. Although this event occurred over twenty years ago, I have winced whenever I have thought of it until I looked at it in more detail. This is what happened:

I was on an airplane with my son, Michael, who was maybe three at the time. This was back in the days when they not only served food on airplanes but served a full, hot meal. The flight attendant pulled the last hot chicken dinner out of her little cart, plopped it in front of me, and went back for more. I started cutting up the chicken into little pieces with the intention of giving them to my son sitting next to me. We shared a couple of bites, and he was eager for his food. Before I finished cutting more, the flight attendant came back with another dinner, which she put on the tray in front of Michael. He eagerly stuck his fork into the big chicken breast and tried to get the whole thing to his mouth, but it dropped off his fork and onto his little bare leg (he was wearing shorts). He immediately screamed, and I realized that his chicken must be a whole lot hotter than mine. I grabbed at the chicken to get it away from him, but it was so hot I instinctively dropped it—right back onto his little leg. He screamed again and desperately tried to squirm out of his seat belt to get away from the burning food. I grabbed my napkin, picked up the hot chicken, wiped the sauce from my son's leg, and began to dab cold water on the spot. Soon there was a silver-dollar-sized blister forming on his leg where the chicken had dropped. He is now in his twenties and still has the scar.

I felt absolutely terrible, not only because my son was in pain but also because I had been completely unable to hold onto the hot chicken that had burned him. What kind of a mother drops something that hot on her child? I was horrified at my inability to make my fingers respond to the crisis more appropriately. For years whenever I thought of this situation, I knew I was a terrible mother who didn't even love her own son enough to protect him. I just couldn't forgive myself.

As I thought through this experience in the detail I laid out in *Forgiving Ourselves*, I began to realize I was not dealing with a sin, not lacking in charity, and not a terrible mom. Even though my actions caused harm to my child and even though I felt terribly guilty, I had no intention of harming Michael, nor was I doing anything against God's commandments. I desperately wished in that moment that I did not live in a world where innocent children get hurt by others' incompetence or limitations, a world in which I could override my body's self-protective instincts. But my job in that situation was not repentance or self-forgiveness—my job was making peace with the fact that I do live in just such a world. I was not sinful. I was weak.

Now consider another experience that has haunted me for years. Like the previous story, it may or may not sound to you that I did anything all that wrong. I have certainly done far worse things in my life, and I hope far better. This story is not significant because its details reveal how righteous or how wicked I truly am. In fact, it is not a story about behavior at all but a story about the importance of our heart in discerning weakness from sin.

About ten years ago, my daughter Monika and I were driving through Arizona on a short trip. It was January and the weather was cool but certainly not cold. I was wearing the leather jacket my husband had bought for me on a trip to Turkey. Even in Turkey this was an expensive jacket, and I loved it for its buttery texture and soft green color.

As we drove along a rural highway, chatting and enjoying the sunshine, our eyes were suddenly riveted to a car flipped over on its roof by the side of the road. The driver had apparently taken a turn too fast and lost control of the vehicle. We were among the first to arrive at the scene as two men were freeing the young woman driver from the smashed car and laying her down on the brown dirt at the side of the road. My daughter is an EMT, so she immediately ran over to help. She asked me to stand back a little to model for others not to crowd in.

The young woman who had been driving had many cuts from the smashed windshield, and she was bleeding a lot. She was crying and afraid. Monika quickly checked her over while the men called 911. Despite all the blood, it appeared that her cuts were mostly superficial and that she had no serious injuries. Monika was worried, however, that the young woman would go into shock.

She explained her concern to the gathering group and asked if anyone had a blanket or a coat to cover the young woman. No one responded. Monika looked at me.

I, of course, knew I had a coat on that I could offer: my beautiful, expensive, green leather coat from my husband. I knew that giving this young accident victim my coat would ruin it. (I don't think you can get blood out of a leather coat.) I knew that I had no other coat to wear for the rest of our trip. I knew it was not that cold out and that this young woman was not in danger of freezing. I saw Monika look at me. And I said nothing.

I hoped she would think I just didn't even think about the fact that I had on a coat, but I knew better. I knew my daughter knew I had made a choice. Shortly someone in the crowd remembered he had a blanket in the car, and he ran off to get it. The young woman's immediate needs were met. The ambulance arrived, and rescuing care was provided. We got back in our car to continue our journey. All was well.

Except in my heart. I have thought about this experience many times. I have rationalized my decision. Even though I felt bad about not being more charitable, I have reminded myself that no one was hurt, no harm done by my choice. I have remembered that I had no other coat, that someone else helped, and I've even thought that had I been the car crash victim bleeding by the roadside, I would never have wanted someone to ruin an expensive coat for me. But I have not been at peace.

Recently I "watched" this scene again in my mind, replaying the options, the feelings, the excuses, the decision. I still was not sure even yet if I had acted out of weakness or out of sin. Maybe even neither? Was it really worth ruining a good coat for someone I didn't know who was not in mortal danger? If I had it to do over again, would I really have done it differently? I didn't think so. Why then, was I still troubled? I was hesitant to ask God for clarification in this matter because I did not really want to hear that He might require such a sacrifice of me.

The Lord must have noticed my consternation, prolonged for so many years. The Spirit gently, kindly, but clearly whispered, "Wendy, whatever happened to that coat?" I recalled I had given it away when it became somewhat worn and out of style. The Spirit continued, "You don't even own this coat any more, this coat you were trying so hard to keep clean. But you are still carrying this woman's blood on your soul."

I began to weep. The question at hand was not whether I owed it to this woman or to my daughter or to God to give away my coat. The question at hand was who was I? Was I a person of charity who would act in Christ's name to comfort a child of God, or did I leave it to someone else to show compassion for a stranger? Was it worth the years of self-doubt and excuse-making I had endured in my effort to hang onto a coat I no longer even owned? The answer was simple: No.

In an odd way I felt no condemnation from the Lord in this exchange. But I also realized that, for me, ignoring my daughter's plea for a coat to help a woman in need was a sin. The bleeding woman may not have been harmed by my failure, but I was harmed. I did not act from a charitable heart. I acted instead to deceive.

It is very hard for me to tell this story. In fact I have never before told it. It is hard because I am ashamed of my choice but even more because I am deeply sorrowful about my unrighteous intent. It is also hard because I have not been completely sure I would have more charity, more courage now than I did then. But I believe that I would, precisely because I now more clearly understand the nature of the choice I was making, the substance of charity, and the blessings of a clean heart.

I do not want to imply that the gospel of Jesus Christ always requires us to respond to a given problem in the same way or that someone else acting as I did would always be wrong. But I do want to imply that I have come to conclude that for me in that moment, my behavior was sinful. I did not act out of love but out of self-interest. If it had been my daughter lying bleeding at the side of the road, the cost of my coat would not even have crossed my mind. I would have stripped it off without a second thought. But this was my sister. Had Christ come across this accident scene, He would have seen this young woman as His responsibility and His opportunity for empathy and care. I did not.

If I were to face such a choice again, I hope I would at least have the compassion and honesty to say to my daughter and to this young woman, "I have a coat, and I have great concern for you. You are welcome to my coat if that is the best option we have. Of course I would rather not ruin my coat if there is another alternative, but you are more important than a coat." I hope I would at least be able to say that. And mean it.

This is why outward criteria do not always work very well when we are trying to distinguish sin from weakness. In the first experience my son was hurt by my action, and in the second my action caused no harm, but that has no bearing on which was sin and which was weakness. In both situations I felt guilty and ashamed for years, but on more careful self-assessment, I dropped all my guilt about the first experience and knew my guilt was warranted in the second. The difference has nothing to do with external outcomes. It has to do with my heart.

The story of the good Samaritan is prompted by a simple question: "Who is my neighbor?" This question follows an exchange in which a lawyer asks the Savior what a person has to do to gain eternal life. I've asked that question as well and with similar intent:

Just how much do I *really* have to do to "make it"? How much can I get away with not doing before I get "demoted" as a slacker?

The Savior does not answer this question but asks the lawyer what he thinks. He asks us as well, and, like the lawyer, we ultimately know the answer: Love the Lord with all our heart, soul, strength, and mind, and our neighbor as ourselves (see Matthew 22:35–40). We know that on these two commandments "hang all the law" (Matthew 22:40). In other words, they are the ultimate criteria for every moral decision, every determination about what is weakness and what is sin. Do we love the Lord most, and with all our soul? Do we believe Him? Do we trust Him? And then, do we love our neighbor as ourselves?

Like me, the man in the story wanted to "justify himself" as he asked, "Who is my neighbour?" (Luke 10:29). We ponder this question as well—with so many needs in the world, who exactly do we have to take care of? What exactly is required? How much do we have to do? Surely I can't be expected to feed and clothe the whole world, so where does my obligation end?

So the Savior tells us a story. There is a man, making a journey from Jerusalem down to Jericho. Jerusalem is the Holy City, high on a hill. Jericho, by the shores of the Dead Sea, is 400 feet below sea level, perhaps the lowest city on earth. I think the details matter, for we too have left a holy city on a long journey down to a lower realm—down, in fact, to the lowest places of earth. This is not just "a" story. This is our story. We are the lonely traveler, making our way through dangerous territory. We too have been stripped of our protective raiment of light, battered and wounded by the thieves of this world, and left spiritually "half-dead" by the side of the road. The priest and Levite of the law of Moses—the law of carnal commandments and outward obedience—do nothing for us in our fallen state. They come, they look, but they pass by on the other side. As do we when we are preoccupied with outward conformity alone.

And then a Samaritan comes along. The Samaritans were despised by the Jews, bringing to mind the description of the Savior as one who "is despised and rejected of men; a man of sorrows, and acquainted with grief" who "hath borne our griefs, and carried our sorrows," "wounded for our transgressions, . . . bruised for our iniquities" (Isaiah 53:3–5). This Samaritan "came where he was: and when he saw him, he had compassion on him, and went to him" (Luke 10:33–34). He does not just look at the wounded man; he *sees* him. He has compassion. He goes to him. He cleanses and anoints and binds up his wounds, then takes him to an inn and takes care of him. He pays the host to continue his care with the words, "Take care of him; and whatsoever thou spendest more, when I come again, I will repay thee" (Luke 10:35). Is not the inn reminiscent of the house of God, the healing hospital for our soul, where our spiritual wounds are cleansed, anointed, and dressed, protective clothing returned, the dreadful work of the thieves of this world redeemed? And is not Christ the one who pays the full price for our healing?

So who is the host, we might wonder? To whom does the Savior hand us as he tries to rescue us from this world's wounding? To one another, of course. And in doing so—and this is important—He promises to fully repay us for all we do for one another in His name. As hosts, we are not the losers here, the ones who give away what matters to us. We are fully, lovingly repaid for all we do in our effort to be worthy of the name of Christ.

We are all among the wounded. We are all commissioned as caring hosts. He is the Healer for us all.

As the story ends, Jesus turns to the lawyer and asks a question, a slightly different question than the one that prompted the story: "Which now of these three, thinkest thou, was neighbour unto him that fell among the thieves?" (Luke 10:36). The question is not about determining the legalistically required object of our responsibility. The question is about us. Not, "Who is my neighbor?" but "Who am I?" Am I a neighbor? Am I a person of charity and compassion? The answer to this question does not focus on who out there among my neighbors is deserving, but on the state of my own heart.[2]

The lawyer answers, "He that shewed mercy on him." Jesus replies, "Go, and do thou likewise" (Luke 10:37). In essence, "Go, and do as I would do. I, the despised Samaritan. Be as I would be."

So there I am, standing by the side of the road, looking on a bleeding woman in need, but like the priest and the Levite, not really seeing her, not going to her. Evaluating my duty according to the law but not allowing my heart to be moved by compassion and mercy. Perhaps if I had had more time to reflect, to weigh all the pros and cons, I could have acted more appropriately, more in keeping with my chosen values. But regardless of my behavior, this moment's urgency revealed the state of my heart and found me wanting.

Weakness? Yes. Preoccupied with the things of this world, rushed, limited, I was not up to the challenge of being like my Savior. I weep to realize how far the distance is between The Great I Am and who I am.

Sin? That too. I acted to deceive, to feign ignorance of the very coat on my back so as to avoid losing it. I was proud of my daughter for her mercy, but I withheld my own. I did not love my neighbor as myself.

As I see myself more clearly from the perspective of many years, I am at long last brokenhearted. I see how I participated in my own deception. I feel naked, blind. The Savior comes to where I am. He sees me, has compassion on me, binds up my wounds, pays Himself the full price of my care. His healing effort applies to me as well. He is gentle and kind. He says, "Go, and do thou likewise."

BELIEVING GOD

There is always a price to be paid when we choose to believe Satan over God, as I did in the previous situation. In the moment of decision, I believed the voice in my head that told me I would miss my coat, that it was too expensive to ruin for "nothing," that I would regret giving it away. But in the end that voice lied. I gave away the coat anyway some years later, but I could never give away the view of myself as one who did not act in love. The Spirit spoke the truth: I avoided getting blood on my coat, but I have carried it for years on my soul.

The commandments are not given to us to trip us up or to fail everyone except the very most pious. They are given to tell us the truth—about what is real, what will make us happy, what will result in good. From the beginning, Satan has whispered to the children of Adam and Eve, "Believe it not; and they believed it not, and they loved Satan more than God. And men began from that time forth to be carnal, sensual, and devilish" (Moses 5:13). Ultimately, every moral choice we make is a choice to believe Satan or to believe God.

In our weak, mortal state, we cannot do all good all the time. We do not have God's unlimited power, energy, or wisdom. King Benjamin in the Book of Mormon mercifully counsels, "And see that all these things are done in wisdom and order; for it is not requisite that a man should run faster than he has strength" (Mosiah 4:27). But when, in our poverty of time and energy, those in need put out their hands to us, this righteous king speaks to us not of our behavior but of our hearts, "I would that ye say in your hearts that: I give not because I have not, but if I had I would give" (Mosiah 4:24).

It is not always easy for us to know when we are justifying ourselves in sin, or when we are conceding our own limitations and weakness. I have learned that for me, sinful impulses are often accompanied by attempts to hide or deceive, by selfish motives, materialism, feelings of inferiority or superiority, worry about what others will think, resentment, defensiveness, and judgmental thoughts. When I am honestly acknowledging my weakness, I am humble, teachable, nondefensive, willing to learn, open to suggestions and help, meek, patient, kind, and earnestly seeking to improve. When I am not sure if I am justifying myself in sin or justified by God despite my weakness, these questions help me parse out what is real.

Ultimately, God will lead me to the answers as I study it out, seek wise counsel from others, and ask Him. But perhaps the hardest thing in this process for me personally is that I have to be willing to know the answer. For years I resisted sorting out whether I was weak or sinful for not giving away my coat. I wanted to justify what I had done because I didn't know where it would end if God really expected me to pass out my clothing to every person who had less than I. But it does end. God cares for me too. He wants my well-being as much as anyone else's. He does not ask me to give everything away but to trust that what I most need and desire is His alone to give. He asks me to allow my heart to be full of charity without fear that somehow it will cost me more than I can afford. I can trust Him fully to care for my heart, my soul, my strength, my mind—the very things He asks of me.

In the past I've been afraid of Satan's lie that God will be like my swimming teacher when I was a child, always stepping back a few more steps and a few more steps until I panic about my ability to stay afloat. But I have changed my mind (see Bible Dictionary, "Repentance").[3] With Nephi, I know in whom I have trusted (see 2 Nephi 4:19). God can be counted on to always tell me the truth about what, in any situation, will make me happy in the long run. What will make me more like Him. Yes, He will always ask more of me than I, in my weak and fallen state, can give. But He can be counted on to make weak things strong. His grace is sufficient to empower us to do—and to be—good.

To those who have struggled as I have to trust the Lord with my all, the Savior said, "Wherefore, settle this in your hearts, that ye will do the things which I shall teach, and command you" (JST Luke 14:28). He invites us to that settled place not to overpower us or prove us inadequate but because it is a place of healing and refuge for our broken hearts.

Chapter 4

HUMILITY: THE "REPENTANCE" FOR WEAKNESS

Almost ironically, weaknesses make us vulnerable to one very dangerous sin: pride. Pride is the quality that responds to weakness and sin with self-deception and insistence that there is no problem at all. When we are proud, we puff ourselves up or we try to hide. We justify our weaknesses and sins, blame other people for them, or get defensive about them. Paradoxically, pride can also lead to excessive shame, a sort of "reverse pride"—a belief that we should be free from weakness and better than other people. With pride we make way too big a deal about our weakness or not nearly a big enough deal, we coddle ourselves or beat ourselves up, we get irritable with others for their weakness, and in general we completely miss the whole point of weakness, which is to teach us humility and charity.

Pride may well be the mother of all sins. President Ezra Taft Benson's classic general conference talk on the dangers of pride[1] has a place of honor in my personal scriptures for this very reason. Pride is a problem because it leads us to sin—which almost always boils down to ignoring God's counsel or thinking it doesn't apply to us because we know better than God what we need, what would make us happy, or what is fair and reasonable. Pride is also a problem because it prevents God from making proper use of our weakness. God is patient and generous with all our weakness with this caveat: that we be humble and have faith in Him. If we are humble and trust Him, He can make weak things become strong unto us. If we are prideful and trust ourselves, the adversary will work hard to make weak things become sin unto us. It is that simple.

Humility is what the Lord prescribes as the antidote to weakness. Humility is probably the mother of all virtues. I think of humility as the "other repentance." I'll explain. Repentance is the antidote to sin, the remedy when we find ourselves on the side of sin (diagram 3, chapter 1). Humility is the antidote to weakness. Many of us are not clear about exactly what humility includes. In this chapter we'll look at the qualities of humility and then at some steps we can take to enact humility in response to weakness. As we are humble in response to our weakness, we qualify for God's promised gift of grace. James teaches, "God resisteth the proud, but giveth grace unto the humble" (James 4:6).

MEEKNESS

As described in the scriptures, humility seems to entail two qualities: being meek and being teachable. Meekness seems to be an attitude of the heart. It includes being submissive to God, easily entreated by others, modest about our accomplishments, gentle, forgiving, and kind. God, the Omnipotent and Omniscient, is meek. The description Jesus gives of himself is "I am meek and lowly in heart" (Matthew 11:29). We can cultivate meekness by reflecting on God's graciousness and compassion for us in our weakness, as well as by considering the example of Jesus Christ.

I have never forgotten a story I heard years ago about a young husband who wanted to buy a house. He and his wife narrowed their choices to two homes. One was a nice home that needed some work and was comfortably within their price range. The second was more the house of their dreams but also more of a stretch financially. They could qualify for a loan to cover the more expensive house and they liked it much better, but there was no question the mortgage payment would take a big chunk out of their paycheck. The young man prayed sincerely for help with this important decision. He knew the first house was more manageable on their current budget, but he worried that in a few years when they were earning more, they would regret not having bought the house of their dreams. He knew the bigger mortgage would mean sacrifice for a time, but he wondered if the sacrifice would be worth it in the long run. As he prayed, a distinct impression formed in his mind in response: "Maybe you should ask someone else. I'm not very ambitious."

To me this story exemplifies the remarkable meekness of God. God did not chastise the young man for his ambition but labeled it for what it was, helping him see more clearly the real issue underlying his confusion. Nor did God tell him what to do or scold him for asking for help. God simply, meekly, disqualified himself as a good advisor on an issue that had more to do with the weakness of ambition than a matter of right or wrong.

Being meek means we are soft, submissive to God, gentle, modest, and nondefensive. It is an attitude more than a specific behavior. It does not mean we are without confidence or personal power. In fact, the only traits Jesus Christ ascribes to himself in scripture are meekness and lowliness of heart, yet He was a man of great boldness when occasion required it. Human meekness acknowledges our weakness—our nothingness before God, our complete reliance upon Him, and our dependence on the patience and charity of others.

Meekness is both a product and a cultivator of deep gratitude, as we recognize how much God blesses us and how indebted we are to him. Meekness is a state of heart.

BEING TEACHABLE

Being teachable, the second quality of humility, may be more a state of mind. It means we are inquisitive, receptive to new ideas, and patient with the process of learning and growth. It includes practicing skills to reduce mistakes and increase our stamina and agility. It includes being open to the help, suggestions, and correction of others. When we are teachable, we acknowledge our need for emotional support, skills training, and instruction. When we are teachable, we know that we do not have all the answers, that others have perspectives and information we lack, and that we need to listen, ask questions, think things through, test out new approaches, and evaluate the results. We are curious about and flexible with others who have a different perspective. The teachable person is resilient in the face of obstacles and setbacks because he or she is more interested in learning than in defending ego or avoiding the pain of failure.

In a recent Sunday School class, we discussed the importance of teaching our children gospel principles. We quickly realized that effective teaching requires something besides skillful explanations or interesting stories. For a teaching interaction to be effective, the learner has to be teachable. Class members were eager to acknowledge that children are not always teachable. We realized that we all become more teachable as we see models *in our teachers* of nondefensiveness, openness to others' ideas, inquisitiveness, respect, and a soft heart. We realized that as parents we need to model these qualities of being teachable so our children can learn to be teachable as well.

The lesson included the following story from Elder F. Enzio Busche of the Seventy: "One day when circumstances made it necessary for me to be at home at an unusual time, I witnessed from another room how our eleven-year-old son, just returning from school, was directing ugly words towards his younger sister. They were words that offended me—words that I had never thought our son would use. My first natural reaction in my anger was to get up and go after him. Fortunately, I had to walk across the room and open a door before I could reach him, and I remember in those few seconds I fervently prayed to my Heavenly Father to help me to handle the situation. Peace came over me. I was no longer angry.

"Our son, being shocked to see me home, was filled with fear when I approached him. To my surprise I heard myself saying, 'Welcome home, son!' and I extended my hand as a greeting. And then in a formal style I invited him to sit close to me in the living room for a personal talk. I heard myself expressing my love for him. I talked with him about the battle that every one of us has to fight each day within ourselves.

"As I expressed my confidence in him, he broke into tears, confessing his unworthiness and condemning himself beyond measure. Now it was my role to put his transgression in the proper perspective and to comfort him. A wonderful spirit came over us, and we ended up crying together, hugging each other in love and finally in joy. What could have been a disastrous confrontation between father and son became, through the help from the powers above, one of the most beautiful experiences of our relationship that we both have never forgotten."[2]

We reflected as a class on the qualities and actions of Elder Busche that had helped his son become teachable. Elder Busche had prayed for help, had been patient and kind, and had invited his son to a private room for a personal talk, giving him time to reflect and mentally prepare. He sat close to his son and extended his love. Perhaps most important, he joined his son in the battle for self-control and integrity rather than consigning him to the losing army. He didn't speak to him of "your problem" but of "the battle every one of us has."

A class member, Grant, then shared an experience that had just occurred in his home. Grant's teenage son and his friends were "maximizing their talents" as computer game wizards. They spent more and more time every day engrossed in the latest and greatest computer game until they talked of little else. Their ingenuity, skill, and enthusiasm were, in a word, *awesome!*

Grant began to notice, however, that he was not seeing much of his son, who was always holed up in the basement on the computer. He hoped the boys would tire of the game and that their enthusiasm would wane. But it did not. In fact, in a stroke of genius they animatedly gathered outdated computers from Grant's office and hooked them all up to each other in elaborate ways so they could all play the game at once.

Grant's concern grew. He had seen young people ruin their lives with addictions to lesser things. He decided something had to be done. He approached his son (undoubtedly in the middle of a crucial battle at Level 38) and asked to speak to him. He led his son to a room where they could speak privately. He sat near him and looked him in the eye. Grant wasn't sure how to begin, but as he felt his love for his son and his concern for his well-being, he started to tear up. He finally said simply, "Son, how is this helping you prepare for a mission?"

This question not only went to the heart of the issue but went to the heart of his son's most righteous and worthy desires. Grant and his son have a good relationship, built up over a long time, and Grant drew on that close connection at this important juncture.

They talked. They cried together. And they came up with a plan. Grant's wife and other sons supported the plan. So the next morning, a Sunday, with light hearts and good humor, they unhooked all the computers, carried them to the church dumpster, and threw them in.

This is not the solution that would have worked in every situation or even been possible or appropriate. But Grant's boys learned that he was willing to join them in the sacrifice required to help them in whatever way was necessary to control their weakness and build on their truest desires and strengths. This was a powerful lesson to all of us in Sunday School that day.

The sons in both of these stories were more teachable because their fathers modeled meekness, love, and respect in interacting with them. Both fathers joined their sons in the battle against human weakness rather than distancing themselves from them, scolding, lecturing, or belittling. This is how I imagine God approaching us in our weakness as well—with meekness, love, and honesty. We can practice being meek and gentle with ourselves as well as we try to learn to be more open, receptive, and teachable. Opening our hearts to God's meekness with us—His kindness, compassion for our weakness, and straightforward expectations unsullied by shaming— reinforces our desire to become more teachable.

Diagram 6 summarizes common differences in approach between humility and pride.

THE SEVEN P's OF HUMILITY

Being meek and teachable gives us a great start on the attitudes of humility, the "other repentance." Like repentance, humility also involves regret, apology, and restitution. Unlike repentance for sin, humility in the face of weakness means acknowledging that although

HUMILITY	PRIDE
Has an attitude of gratitude	Holds an attitude of entitlement
Is teachable and inquisitive	Is dogmatic and resistant to new ideas
Remains open, willing to yield to others	Is closed to alternatives; needs to be right
Works to stay connected to others	Isolates real self from others
Emphasizes contributing and growing	Focuses on (conspicuous) consumption
Desires to serve and help	Is preoccupied with self-interest
Is self-aware and working to improve	Compares self to others and works to win
Is willing to repent and let go	Has a hard heart and turns away from God
Sees the big picture but works on today's problems today	Lives for momentary satisfaction and postpones problem-solving for tomorrow
Accepts and addresses weaknesses	Denies and tries to hide from weaknesses

Diagram 6: Humility or Pride

we would like to, we will not simply walk away from our weakness and "never do it again." Let's talk about the Seven P's of humility: Ponder, Prioritize, Pace, Practice, Prop Up, Patience, and Pray. In these processes we will learn and improve, get help from others and from the Spirit, and change gradually over time.

Ponder. Just as repentance begins with recognition of our sin, humility begins as we ponder our weakness. Self-honesty does not just happen. It takes courage to come to God in our weakness and see it for what it is. We should ponder not only what our specific weaknesses might include but also how they interfere with our truest goals, how much they bother people we love, how they keep us from what matters most to us, and how they distance us from other people. As we ponder we invite feedback from others, including the Holy Spirit, about what we need to work on. We stop ignoring the extent of our weakness or the dangers of it, instead opening our hearts and minds to information.

Pondering includes turning "into" our weakness instead of turning away. We face the weakness head on, talk about it honestly, analyze what happened and how we can learn, and make plans to improve. Not only does that help us grow but it helps us get along. I love the following example of turning "into" a weakness:

"Three twelve-year-olds are heading to a soccer field for gym class. Two athletic-looking boys are walking behind—and snickering at—the third, a somewhat chubby classmate.

"'So you're going to *try* to play soccer,' one of the two says sarcastically to the third, his voice dripping with contempt.

"It's a moment that, given the social code of these middle-school boys, can easily escalate into a fight.

"The chubby boy closes his eyes for a moment and takes a deep breath, as though steeling himself for the confrontation that lies ahead.

"Then he turns to the other two and replies, in a calm, matter-of-fact voice, 'Yeah, I'm going to try—but I'm not very good at it.'

"After a pause he adds, 'But I'm great at art—show me anything and I can draw it real good. . . .'

"Then, pointing to his antagonist, he says, 'Now you—*you're* great at soccer, really fantastic! I'd like to be that good someday, but I'm just not. Maybe I can get a little better at it if I keep try-ing.'

"At that, the first boy, his disdain now utterly disarmed, says in a friendly tone, 'Well, you're not really *that* bad. Maybe I can show you a few things about how to play.'"[3]

What a masterful display of humility and "turning in" to aware-ness of a weakness instead of defending against it. This young man's humility not only disarms a foe but makes a friend.

Elder F. Enzio Busche describes a place of prayerful, soul-level pondering that leads to both repentance of sin and humility for our weakness: "Initiated by the hearing of the word of truth, a dis-ciple of Christ is therefore constantly, even in the midst of all regu-lar activities, striving all day long through silent prayer and con-templation to be in the depth of self-awareness to keep him in the state of meekness and lowliness of heart. It is the prophet Mormon who points out that 'because of meekness and lowliness of heart cometh the visitation of the Holy Ghost, which Comforter filleth with hope and perfect love' (Moro. 8:26).

"With this enlightened understanding of the deadly battle-front inside of us, we are painfully aware that we can only ask for and receive the help of the Lord, as the God of truth, under the con-dition of complete and relentless self-honesty. . . .

"Enlightened by the Spirit of truth, we will then be able to pray for the increased ability to endure truth and not to be made angry by it (see 2 Ne. 28:28). In the depth of such a prayer, we may finally be led to that lonesome place where we suddenly see ourselves naked in all soberness. Gone are all the little lies of self-defense. We see ourselves in our vanities and false hopes for car-nal security. We are shocked to see our many deficiencies, our lack of gratitude for the smallest things. We are now at that sacred place that seemingly only a few have courage to enter."[4]

Elder Terrence C. Smith, a member of the Seventy, points out that the Holy Ghost is the Comforter, but surely He does not comfort us in our sins. He *can* comfort us, however, when we respond to adversity and weakness with meekness and lowliness of heart.[5]

Prioritize. Recognizing that weakness includes limitations on our time, energy, and emotional reserves, we understand that we cannot tackle all our individual weaknesses at once. We prayerfully consider what we most need to work on now. We may want to develop a skill, instill a new habit or reduce an old one, tackle a new project, or reduce a character flaw. Priorities help us focus our energy on what matters most today.

In our longing for God, we want to know what He would have us do and become. Our priority is to learn His priority for us. In humility we also acknowledge that trying to do everything at once is self-defeating. Even though it can feel good to set a lot of goals that give us the illusion of progress, we really can do only a limited number of things at a time.

My husband is masterful at this. I want to set ten goals at a time to relieve my discomfort with all the things I see wrong with me. I feel better while setting the goals but worse when I burn out on them almost as fast as I set them. Dave is much more realistic and less shame-driven about change. He works on dozens of projects at once, but when he is ready to tackle personal change he sets one goal at a time, devotes considerable time and energy to it, and generally gets the job done, even if it takes years.

Dave also reminds me of the importance of starting with the "low-hanging fruit" of small, simple changes to begin a "virtuous cycle" of success. Sometimes we are well served to begin with small, manageable changes that are relatively easy to make. As we gain skill and confidence, tackling bigger aspects of our mortal weakness feels more doable.

Elder Neal A. Maxwell of the Quorum of the Twelve writes: "Striking the proper balance is one of the keenest tests of our agency. Therefore, we need to ask regularly for inspiration in the use of our time and in the making of our daily decisions. So often our hardest choices are between competing and desirable alternatives (each with righteous consequences), when there is *not* time to do both at once. Indeed, it is at the mortal intersections—where time and talent and opportunities meet—that priorities, like traffic lights, are sorely needed."[6]

Pace. Elder Maxwell also invites us to careful pacing of our energy and effort. He reminds us: "Given our weaknesses . . . paced progress is essential, much as God used six measured and orderly creative periods (followed by respite) in preparing man and this earth. There is a difference, therefore, between being steadily and effectively or 'anxiously' engaged, on the one hand, and, on the other hand, being frantically engaged one moment and being passive and detached the next."[7]

Elder Maxwell reminds us that the Lord's invitations to retire to bed early (see D&C 88:124), to rest on the Sabbath day (see Exodus 20:9–10), and to "not run faster or labor more than you have strength and means" (D&C 10:4) speak to our need to pace ourselves in His work. Our mortal bodies are limited by time, space, and the constraints of hunger, fatigue, and ignorance. While we can push ourselves to do remarkable things when necessary, we also pay a price in lowered immunity, more susceptibility to temptation, and decreased energy afterwards. We need intervals of rest and renewal after such expenditures. In general, a steady pace of consistent effort is the most effective and efficient course.

Practice. When working on a weakness, we don't just change our mind and the rest follows. We will need to practice the new skills we are trying to develop. A professional pianist spends hours every day practicing the piano. Not only is he learning new music for upcoming concert tours but he is constantly trying to improve his technique to both reduce wear and tear on his hands and increase his options for expressing the music. Likewise, our need for practice in managing our anger, improving our time management, maintaining motivation for scripture reading, or helping our children with homework effectively is not a sign that we are inept or unspiritual—it is a sign of our commitment to our music.

As a mission president's wife, I learned that missionaries were sometimes confused by how hard it could be to discern the Spirit. Having had clear spiritual witnesses of important truths or guidance in important matters, they assumed that God's language, "Spirit," was their native tongue, one they should instinctively understand. Because they knew how to say and understand, *"Bonjour, comment allez-vous?"* in Spirit, they sometimes thought they had the whole language down. When they missed or misunderstood a spiritual prompting, they wondered if they were unworthy or even foolish to believe God had ever spoken to them.

We decided that the language of the Spirit is more sophisticated and subtle than we first thought. Like arriving in the field to realize that one's French is not quite as fluent as it felt in the MTC, we began to realize that we need experience and practice to discern the subtleties of the language of God. We would need to work hard, study, and learn from our mistakes in both comprehension and expression. As we did so we would be able to discern more accurately and consistently, and God would be able to communicate to us more and more subtle and sophisticated ideas.

Practice is an important part of any humble effort at managing a weakness or learning a skill.

Prop up. When we are truly humble, we know we can do so little by ourselves. Just fixing myself a piece of toast means I must depend on many other people who plant, grow, harvest, sort, clean, package, prepare, bake, transport, and market the bread I will eat. That doesn't even get into the number of people it takes to produce the toaster oven with all its components or the electricity to run it. A simple piece of toast probably reflects the work of thousands of people, all helping me get breakfast. It also reflects the bounteous goodness and blessings of a loving Father in Heaven who provides us all with sun and air and life.

Fixing ourselves is at least as complicated as fixing toast. We need people to teach us, encourage us, support us, and model for us. Humility means we acknowledge this interdependence. We listen to people who know what we do not. We read and study their research and experience. We let others show us how and appreciatively accept their tutoring. We watch their example and actively try to learn from it. We invite their encouraging words and supportive actions. And we gladly provide all of these things for others. People who help and teach us *prop up* our efforts to change and grow.

Even more than we need others, we need God to sustain, befriend, and direct us. Without the gifts of the Holy Ghost and the grace made available through the Atonement of Jesus Christ, our efforts to grow and change will always fall woefully and utterly short. No matter how much we try, learn, or improve, we will never be like God without the application of His grace to our lives.

In addition to God and other people, we also prop up ourselves with plans and goals, calendars and budgets, rewards and reminders, study and seeking. When writing my first book, I had a family of teenagers and a busy life. I had a love–hate relationship with writing; it was stressful and demanding, yet I wanted to do it. I got a calendar, bought some alphabet stickers of exotic zoo animals (I'm serious), and put a sticker on the calendar each time I wrote for an hour. My goal was to get through the alphabet each month. I no longer need stickers to get myself to write, but I still need my walking partner's encouragement, my husband's strong organizational sense, the objective eye of good editors, and the professional and personal input of many people to get my words on paper. Whether learning to write, visit teach, eat healthy, be less critical, or enjoy the temple, I benefit from many props: the help of many capable people, my own careful plans and goals, and, sometimes, exotic animal stickers.

Patience. Patience is a key quality of humility. God promised the Saints in Ohio in 1831 that remarkable blessings awaited them as they stripped themselves of jealousy, fear, and pride. But He acknowledged that preparation for these blessings would take time and require patience:

"Ye are not able to abide the presence of God now, neither the ministering of angels; wherefore, continue in patience until ye are perfected" (D&C 67:13).

God does not enjoin us to patience with our sins. He is uniformly urgent about our need for repentance. But He does invite us to be patient with the process of perfection. Perfection is not flawlessness; it is a state of spiritual maturity, wholeness, and development. It requires learning, risk taking, resilience, and patience.

When I think of patience, I imagine someone who does not become discouraged or irritable when things take longer than anticipated. I note that this definition of patience asks us to make peace with the future—the far-distant day when the current problem will be overcome or the current crisis resolved. Ironically, the patient person is not preoccupied with the future but lives thoroughly in the present. Patience teaches us that this precise moment is tolerable. As we respond to what this moment requires of us, the future will take care of itself. I don't have to resist temptation forever—just right now. I don't have to practice forever—just right now. I don't have to endure another's provocative behavior forever—just right now.

And "just right now" is always endurable. As I "continue in patience" to take one day at a time, one obstacle at a time, God can teach me and help me develop.

Prayer. The seventh P, integral to all the rest, is prayer. Humility acknowledges our absolute dependence on the Lord for the spiritual gifts (such as faith, hope, charity, healing, teaching, tongues, wisdom, administration, discernment, and revelation) we need in order to adequately compensate for our weaknesses and become more like the Savior. We obtain these gifts through humble, sincere, and constant prayer. They are contingent upon our asking, our pleading with the Lord for them.

I understand this, but my heart is convicted by the following observation from Hugh Nibley, professor emeritus at Brigham Young University: "The [spiritual] gifts are not in evidence today, except for one gift, which you notice the people ask for—the gift of healing. They ask for that with honest intent and with sincere hearts, and we really have that gift, because we are desperate and nobody else can help us. . . .

"As for these other gifts—how often do we ask for them? How earnestly do we seek for them? *We could have them if we did ask, but we don't. 'Well, who denies them?' Anyone who doesn't ask for them.*"[8]

Not by casual request but by humble, sincere petition, we are granted by God the gifts of the Spirit He promises will compensate for human limitations. When we are as earnest and persistent in our prayer for charity, wisdom, or hope as we are for the gift of healing for one we love, remarkable spiritual power can ensue.

A TALE OF TWO CITIES

After his conversion, Alma the Younger serves for a time as the chief judge of the Nephite nation. He is also the high priest of the Church. Alma becomes convinced he cannot fulfill the duties of high priest adequately while operating as chief judge. Modeling humility for all of us, Alma prioritizes his responsibilities prayerfully and with awareness of his mortal limitations, turns his civic duties over to others, and turns his full attention to teaching the gospel.

Alma 5–7 records his preaching to the two Nephite cities of Zarahemla and Gideon. In Zarahemla sin predominates; in Gideon the people are largely free from sin. He counsels these two cities very differently. It behooves us to reflect prayerfully upon which set of advice is more applicable to us. Do we live in Zarahemla? Or in Gideon?

The people of Zarahemla, although many are members of the Church, are in a sinful state, and Alma calls them to repentance. He speaks to them of their sins: violence, pride, envy, persecuting other people, materialism, turning their backs on the poor, and all manner of wickedness. He asks how they can expect to sit down with Abraham, Isaac, Jacob, and the holy prophets who have been cleansed of sin. He speaks to them of the mighty change of heart that comes as we remember God's goodness; exercise faith and trust in Him; humble ourselves; change our minds, hearts, and behavior; and renew our covenants with God. The people respond. They repent, assemble often to hear the word of God, and fast and pray for the unbelievers. Those who don't are no longer numbered with the Church.

Then Alma goes to the city of Gideon. Preaching there for the first time, he says: "And behold, I have come having great hopes and much desire that I should find that ye had humbled yourselves before God, and that ye had continued in the supplicating of his grace, that I should find that ye were blameless before him, that I should find that ye were not in the awful dilemma that our brethren were in at Zarahemla" (Alma 7:3).

These are not people without weakness—they still need humility and grace—but Alma has great hopes that they are "blameless" before God—without sin. He speaks to them of Christ's coming in weakness—suffering pain, affliction, temptation, sickness, infirmity, and death—that He might know how to succor His people. Alma still invites those among them who are in a state of sin to repent, be baptized, and covenant to keep God's commandments. But he notes that for the most part the people of Gideon are "in the paths of righteousness . . . which lead to the kingdom of God" (Alma 7:19). He invites them to awaken to a sense of their duty to God that they might be "blameless before him, . . . walk[ing] after the holy order of God, after which [they] have been received" (v. 22).

As he continues to preach, we see all the themes we have explored in this chapter regarding humility and teachableness as the appropriate response to weakness: "And now I would that ye should be humble, and be submissive and gentle; easy to be entreated; full of patience and long-suffering; being temperate in all things; being diligent in keeping the commandments of God at all times; asking for whatsoever things ye stand in need, both spiritual and temporal; always returning thanks unto God for whatsoever things ye do receive. And see that ye have faith, hope, and charity, and then ye will always abound in good works. And may the Lord bless you, and keep your garments spotless, that ye may at last be brought to sit down with Abraham, Isaac, and Jacob, and the holy prophets . . . having your garments spotless even as their garments are spotless, in the kingdom of heaven to go no more out" (Alma 7:23–25). The people of Gideon are not without weakness. But they are clean, "spotless." And in that state God blesses them with peace (see v. 27).

Undoubtedly we all have at least a time-share condominium in Zarahemla. I believe, however, that many members of the Church have their regular residence in Gideon. We are not without weakness, but we love the Lord and we trust His love for us, we earnestly do our duty, we are generous with the poor, we are grateful, and we are striving to walk in paths of righteousness with increasing integrity and love. We are clean. And in that state, we have great cause for hope, for joy, for humility, and for peace.

Chapter 5

OVERCOMING SHAME, STRENGTHENING HUMILITY

Making the careful distinction between weakness and sin sparks my hope and courage. I certainly don't want to be coddled in my sins by mislabeling them as weaknesses, but neither do I want to become despondent and hopeless because I think my weaknesses—which I will not fully eliminate in this life—are really sins that I can eliminate. I am energized and more willing to tackle my endless list of weaknesses when I know they do not stand between me and my Father. I can afford to keep trying. I can feel the joy of my redemption.

Just as we can confuse the concepts of *weakness* and *sin*, we often don't distinguish carefully between *shame, guilt, humility,* and *humiliation.* Excessive shame (as I'm defining it here) turns us away from God and those we love. In contrast, mature guilt, or godly sorrow as it is sometimes called in the scriptures, along with true humility (not humiliation), helps us repair and deepen our relationships with God and other people. This is not just a matter of semantics. When we mistake shame for godly sorrow or humiliation for humility, we misunderstand what God expects. We lose our way. And we miss out on much of the healing and peace God longs to give us.

I have come to the conclusion that shame, like pride, involves excessive preoccupation with others' opinions at the expense of reliance on the Lord's opinions. In that sense, I think shame is a counterfeit for the true humility that leads us toward God's grace. We don't always recognize the counterfeit or distinguish it from the genuine humility we know we need. We can think we are being humble when in fact we are succumbing to shame. This chapter is about making that distinction, so we can combat shame and strengthen genuine humility.

On the left side of diagram 7, we note that shame is one of several emotional states that move us toward sin. Godly sorrow, or appropriate guilt, however, is a part of the repentance that turns us away from sin and qualifies us for forgiveness. Genuine humility, as illustrated on the right side of diagram 7, qualifies us for God's grace, turning weakness to strength.

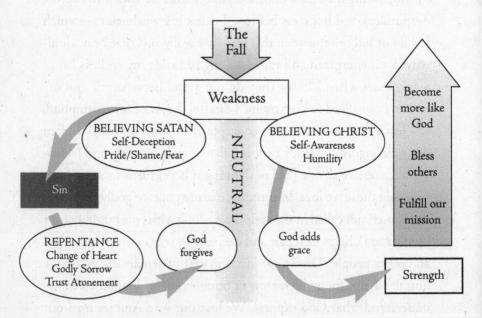

Diagram 7: Weakness, Sin, and Strength

DEFINITIONS

Godly sorrow, or mature guilt, is a constructive emotion. We *are* guilty of sin, and so *feeling* guilty is completely appropriate, including feeling deep remorse for our rebellion against God and sorrow for the hurt we have caused others. Awareness of our guilt is the first step in repentance and change. This godly sorrow appropriately follows the recognition that we have violated our own moral code.

Shame as we will define it here is not necessary to godly sorrow. Shame can even get in the way of godly sorrow or mature guilt. Shame can include self-disdain, fear of others' opinions, or feelings of worthlessness. It is also akin to embarrassment, a tacit agreement with the judgments of others about our inferiority or foolishness. Shame preoccupies us with the opinions of people instead of the opinion of the Lord. To Joseph Smith, God warns, "For behold, you *should not have feared man* more than God" (D&C 3:7; emphasis added). But shame can also make us feel embarrassed before God, turning "divine discontent"[1] over our weaknesses into discouragement or humiliation as we imagine His shaking finger. Even worrying about the opinions of righteous people can distract us from our righteous desires.

Shame is not the only emotional response one can have to weakness. Some people struggle more with pride, anger, fear, worry, timidity, indifference, or some other emotion. But shame is often at least an element in these other emotions and lends them a particularly bitter taste. It is also the emotion we most often confuse with genuine humility or with godly sorrow or mature guilt. For this reason, I think it helps to see some of the important differences between these states.

As we've discussed, weakness is not a cause for shame or self-disdain, either. Although we may feel deep remorse for the pain our weaknesses can cause others, or "divine discontent" about our limitations, humility does not require humiliation. The Savior says to the prophet Jeremiah, worried about his inadequacy before others, "Say not, I am a child: for thou shalt go to all that I shall send thee, and whatsoever I command thee thou shalt speak. *Be not afraid of their faces:* for I am with thee" (Jeremiah 1:7–8; emphasis added).

Unlike humiliation or shame, humility entails awareness of our true relationship with God and our true equality with others. In this awareness we see our utter weakness, our dependency on and distance from the absolute righteousness, power, and wisdom of Deity, but we also trust completely in our absolute worth, in our dignity and value as children of a loving Father. Humility fills us with wonder and awe at the love, patience, and goodness of God, renewing our desire to be closer to Him through discipleship and worship.

DISTINGUISHING SHAME
FROM GODLY SORROW

To further illustrate the difference between shame and godly sorrow, consider the Parable of the Angry Drivers. It goes like this:

Sherry and Gwen both feel bad about losing their temper while driving. Sherry is embarrassed to think someone might have seen her screaming like a third-world military dictator, and she hears her mother's voice in her head asking her what the neighbors will think. She talks back to these voices by telling herself she was justified in getting angry because the other driver was such an idiot. She never wants to see her again, but if she did she would surely give her a piece of her mind. She secretly wonders, however, if what happened was her fault. She can't stop stewing about it, alternately justifying her rage and feeling stupid for it. She feels ashamed and wants the whole mess to just go away.

Gwen is the "other driver." She also feels bad about losing her temper. Once she calms down she realizes that Sherry is just another frazzled motorist like herself who doesn't deserve to be lambasted for simple carelessness. Gwen believes strongly in kindness and self-control, and when she shortchanges herself in these categories, she feels disappointed in her behavior. She reflects on what made her so angry and how she can approach such situations in the future so she won't get so volatile. She asks her husband for suggestions because she really wants to improve. She wishes she knew where Sherry lives so she could apologize. She feels sorry and wants to make it right.

As we see in this parable, both shame and godly sorrow can include uncomfortable feelings about having done something we consider inappropriate or hurting someone else, but that is where

SHAME	GODLY SORROW/ DIVINE DISCONTENT
Creates feelings of embarrassment, worthlessness	Creates feelings of remorse for violating our moral code
Fears being looked down upon for weakness	Desires to improve our weaknesses
Leads to hiding and blaming	Leads to confessing and repairing
Inhibits growth and learning	Enhances growth and learning
Causes self-view to be basically "bad"	Causes self-view to be basically "good"
Desires to hide "badness" from others	Desires to align our behavior with good self-image

Diagram 8: Shame or Godly Sorrow/Divine Discontent

the similarities end. Shame leads people to hide and blame; godly sorrow, or mature guilt, leads people to confess and repair.[2] Shame inhibits growth and esteem, while godly sorrow enhances both, providing an impetus to constructive change. With shame we see ourselves as bad people who have done something embarrassing or humiliating, and because we are inherently bad we want to hide our error so others will think we are better than we think we are. We want our image to be better than our behavior. With mature guilt we see ourselves as good people who have done something against our moral standards, and because we have strong moral values and compassion for others we want to correct the wrong. We want our behavior to be more consistent with our basically positive self-image.

In short, shame makes us want to run and hide, while godly sorrow for our sins or "divine discontent" over our weaknesses makes us want to improve and make things right.

Shame is probably a weakness that comes with the territory of being human. In some settings, carefully bounded, shaming can provide an initial motivation for obedience and social conformity. But shaming is not a good long-term strategy for promoting obedience because it motivates by fear instead of by righteous desire. Most parents use some shaming messages to socialize children and to try to correct unwanted behavior. When we internalize this shame, we may humiliate ourselves as a sort of preemptive strike to beat others to the punch. It takes honesty, courage, and a strong sense of our worth to acknowledge wrongdoing and change without losing hope or self-esteem. Excessive shame undermines all of the above. God is not averse to shaming rebellious souls who don't feel remorse for their sins, but He does not shame us for our weakness when we are trying. The voice of shame is not from Him.

YOU OUGHT *NOT* BE ASHAMED

Because I know shame is not very healthy, I really don't like feeling ashamed. In fact I feel ashamed of feeling ashamed. I have learned as a psychologist that people who become clinically depressed are often those who get depressed about being depressed, just as those who have the biggest problem with anxiety are those who get anxious about being anxious. Likewise, being ashamed of being ashamed only makes shame harder to shake off. When we accept our own emotional states with calmness, curiosity, and compassion, we can learn from our feelings and then let them go. When we get ashamed of our feelings and go overboard trying to suppress or get rid of them, we often make them worse. People who can feel, name, and reflect on their emotions tend to be much better at accepting them, learning from them, and then releasing them.

We don't have to do something awful to feel deep shame. In Lehi's vision of the tree of life, many people come to partake of the fruit that represents the love of God. But not far from the tree is a great and spacious building full of materialistic, prideful people who mock and point their fingers at those who eat from the tree. Many of those who have tasted God's love are subsequently ashamed, and in their shame many of them wander away from the tree and its precious fruit. They don't want to be seen doing something others label foolish (see 1 Nephi 8:24–28). Even when we are doing good things, feelings of shame can undermine our confidence and weaken our resolve.

Lehi's dream suggests that shame and pride are linked. When we draw our self-esteem from the approval of others instead of the love of God, we feel shame when the chorus in our internal great and spacious building points a finger at our weaknesses—or even our valiant behavior when it is not "socially acceptable." So what are the alternatives to shame? When we have a shame attack, we don't have to wander off in embarrassment, nor do we have to join the mocking chorus of pride. We may not be able to topple the great and spacious building completely, but we can learn to turn our back on it and focus instead on the true source of self-esteem: God's fruitful and amazing love. Responding to our weakness with humility leads us toward strength.

COMBATING SHAME

I've found three steps helpful in combating bouts of shame. First, it helps to simply *Name the Shame*. When we see shame for what it is—an uncomfortable but not especially accurate or constructive feeling—we feel less inclined to assume that it means something real about us. We can see it instead as a temptation, an old habit, or a way we learned in the past to beat others to the punch of pointing out our faults. Rather than getting agitated and self-blaming we can get calm, curious, and compassionate. Like the boy in the last chapter who acknowledged his weakness at soccer without losing self-esteem, we can acknowledge our weakness without accepting the derisive opinions of voices of shame.

Next it helps to *Rejoin the Human Race*. Sharing our experience with someone who loves and supports us helps us feel less isolated and alone with our shame. Because the whole point of shame is to shun and exclude us, reconnecting with loving friends combats shame and keeps our foibles in perspective. Reconnecting with people who love us reminds us of our worth and value.

Finally, it helps to *Dissect the Shame*. By analyzing our particular shame vulnerabilities we are better prepared to take appropriate steps to combat them. People can be ashamed of many things. Lane Fischer, professor of counseling psychology at Brigham Young University, outlines six categories of shame along with the feelings and issues that accompany them, which I've adapted here.[3] They include shame for

+ weaknesses we believe others will dislike
+ failures
+ needs or dependencies
+ fears
+ ways we are different
+ our circumstances or history

Most of us have some experience with each of these categories but have one or two we "favor." Because shame can be such a big deterrent to genuine humility and growth, let's look in more detail at these specific sources of shame and how to approach them with genuine humility instead.

Shame about Weakness

In essence, shame about our weakness is shame about being like everyone else: limited, vulnerable, and inadequate. If we draw self-worth from being slightly better than others, being weak, flawed, and imperfect like everybody else threatens our self-esteem. We may become reclusive, boast excessively, or just keep things shallow so others won't know the real us.

We may assume we have to be strong in order for others to like us, but sharing our weaknesses generally brings us closer to others than displaying our strengths. I still remember a story I read decades ago about a young mother, very pregnant, who received a call from her husband's old girlfriend. The girlfriend had not married, was in town on business, and asked if she could drop by for a brief visit. The young mother scrambled to pick up her house and make herself presentable. When the career woman arrived, she was perfectly groomed and coifed and more than a little intimidating to the young mother. After a casual exchange and a brief visit, the career woman stood to leave, and the young mother felt some relief that the visit was almost over. Suddenly the career woman stopped in mid-sentence to stare at the floor. To the young mother's chagrin, the object of her rival's gaze was a large, shriveled, dirt-encrusted piece of orange peel sitting right in the middle of the floor as if it had been there for years. She was mortified.

I don't remember how the young mother dealt with the situation in the moment, but I do remember how she dealt with it after her visitor left. I'm sure it took work for her to get to this point, but she began to reflect on the old orange peel that had betrayed her less-than-perfect life. The young mother remembered bits of conversation suggesting that a career was not the other woman's first choice and that the young mother actually had the life the other woman longed for. She imagined the relief it might have been to the former girlfriend to know that the person she had "lost" to was not perfect. How nice it must have felt to her rival, the young mother concluded, to realize that *her* rival had flaws too. She concluded that instead of the shriveled orange peel being a sign of her failure, it was more like a gift she could give this sister in the gospel to testify of their shared humanity and mutual imperfections. She decided to be grateful for the orange peel.

Humility about Weakness

We can combat our shame about our weakness by remembering that honesty and humility in weakness draw us closer while outward strengths often intimidate, pushing others away. As we join others in our common humanity, we begin to free ourselves of competitiveness, jealousy, and pride. Keeping a sense of humor about the shriveled orange peels in our lives and being open about our weaknesses instead of hiding them can help us more humbly accept the whole of who we are. Such acceptance is a strength of great worth.

SHAME ABOUT FAILURE

When we believe our worth equates to what we can produce, we can feel deep shame about not doing a stellar job at everything we undertake, whether we are raising a child, a garden, or a building. Sometimes this belief morphs into resistance to undertaking our work. After all, who wants to take on a project or relationship when the expectations—and chances of being a disappointment—feel astronomical?

When we believe our worth is bound up in our productivity, the world fills up with "shoulds." Everything can feel like a demand, and resisting all those demands can feel essential to keeping our sanity. We can go quickly from "I'd like to try that" to "I really should do that" to "I have to do it" to "I don't want to do it" to "I hate the whole idea of it." Resentment builds about having to perform. We take on too much; we don't know when to stop. Mistakes or setbacks are not seen as opportunities for learning and growth; they are indictments of our character and worth.

When shame about not doing well pounds at the door, it helps to remember that failure does not mean we are unusually incompetent; it can also mean we are stretching to tackle something difficult or new. As we reconnect with why we want to do something rather than flogging ourselves with "shoulds," we can reconnect with the joy of learning, creating, and playing with problems and ideas. We can practice deep trust that our worth is not based on our performance.

Humility about Failure

My husband can get more done than any ten people I know. He feels disappointed when something doesn't go well, but he is obsessed with learning from mistakes and improving on past performance rather than disintegrating into shame and blame. He works hard to get things right, but he also is very philosophical about failure. He makes time to unwind, to play, and to rest. By doing these things he stays passionate about his work, is highly motivated, and bounces back quickly after setbacks. He stays closely connected to why he *wants* to do what he does rather than depending on "shoulds" to stay motivated. He is focused on learning over blaming.

Feelings of inadequacy, even failure, are the price we all pay to grow and to contribute. If we don't take this risk of trying hard things then we stagnate. The risk is not imaginary, however; sometimes things will not go well. When that happens, it really helps to remember the law of averages. By mathematical definition, half of everything we do will rate below our personal average. This is not a catastrophe worth bemoaning—it is just math. No matter how good we get at something, half of our performances on that task will be below our personal average.

It is an act of courage, strength, and character to care enough about something to give it our best shot, even if our best shot doesn't get us to the Olympics. Mistakes show us where we need to learn, not where we need to hide.

SHAME ABOUT NEEDINESS

As a teenager in the sixties, I learned a fancy word with a bitter taste: *chauvinism*. Male chauvinists were men who didn't like and didn't value women. Years later, a colleague shared her observation that chauvinistic men were actually people who didn't like vulnerability. They hated vulnerability in themselves and distanced themselves from their own vulnerability by despising it in others.

One doesn't have to be a male chauvinist to dislike feeling vulnerable or to feel ashamed of needs or dependency. But pretending we don't have needs is an illusion we can maintain only at the expense of other people who meet our needs without our having to acknowledge, appreciate, or value their service. When they don't meet our needs, we blame them for incompetency rather than owning our dependency and asking for help honestly and humbly. I believe we do this out of shame.

Underneath the illusion of needlessness is often a deep-seated belief that having needs is dishonorable and reduces our personal power. We feel humiliated to recognize how utterly dependent we are on an unseen host of people, both living and beyond the veil, whose labor sustains our life. But when we don't acknowledge the help we receive, we also miss feeling loved and cared for by those who willingly help us. We see their service, if we see it at all, as something they do out of duty or necessity, not love. We mistakenly believe only weak people have needs.

Humility about Neediness

Self-reliance, hard work, and personal strength are valuable characteristics but only when they include humble acknowledgment of our reliance on others. When we deeply remember and appreciate the thousands of people who serve and help us and whose labor sustains us, it need not make us feel powerless and ashamed. It can make us feel grateful and cared for.

Acknowledging our needs and dependency on others does not mean we should sit around waiting to be waited on, nor does it mean disintegrating into helplessness until others act on our behalf. Reducing our shame about our needs helps us honestly acknowledge both our weakness and our power, both our dependency and our gifts for blessing others. We can reduce shame about neediness both by asking for help and by extending it gladly.

SHAME ABOUT FEARS

One of the biggest fears children have to contend with is fear of being abandoned. When we are small and unlearned, we need adults for everything from food to comfort to information to direction. Nothing is more frightening to a vulnerable child than being left, emotionally or physically. For most children this fear of abandonment is soothed by predictable, consistent parenting from people who are emotionally present and invested. But some children are difficult to soothe, face more scary things than most, or have parents who just aren't soothing. They can end up feeling ashamed of both their fears and the strategies they use to combat them.

Humility about Fears

Building strong social networks with people who are calm and consistent, learning the skills of apology and repair, and building routines and structures that provide order and predictability can help us combat fears. As we learn to take better care of ourselves we are less dependent on others to bring consistency and structure to soothe our fears. Shame about our fears can be replaced with respect for how much we have endured. We can afford to see how much in our life is good and safe despite heartache and uncertainty. The humiliation of having been abandoned in our time of need can be replaced by humility at having been helped to survive. Such humility helps us gain the strengths of resilience, compassion, and gratitude for life.

SHAME ABOUT BEING DIFFERENT

I grew up in California where snow is truly a rarity. I raised my children in Michigan, where snow is a way of life. I was amazed to discover by actual observation that snowflakes really are different. This is a wondrous phenomenon. Even more wondrous is the uniqueness of every child of God.

Sometimes, however, we can feel shame about our uniqueness. Our individuality can be a source of embarrassment and misunderstanding. This is common in people who are minorities in some obvious trait, who have disabilities or illnesses, who have lived through trauma, or who grew up outside the predominant culture; it is also common among those who are especially gifted, smart, athletic, attractive, or creative. Because each of us is truly unique, each of us can be ridiculed or belittled for being different in some way.

Humility about Differences

While our differences can separate us, we also all have our uniqueness in common. As we climb out of our self-consciousness about our differences to become curious about the experiences and feelings of others, we find that under surface differences we are deeply similar. We can reduce our envy of others' favored status of "normality."

I am most inclined to envy another's life when I am neglecting my own. When I feel jealous of someone else, I know it is time to refocus my energy on owning my own life, taking the risks to develop my talents and celebrate my uniqueness. This is not easy. It means getting more comfortable with living in the dark, not knowing, and feeling uncertain. It means making room for a little more chaos and a little less certainty in my relationships and my work. But as I do so I feel more at home in my own life and less envious of the comfy home next door. The pointing fingers quiet down a bit, and I am more open to seeing my uniqueness as precious to God instead of problematic.

SHAME ABOUT OUR HISTORY

To forgive is to give up all hope of ever having a better past.[4] Although it seems obvious to the rational mind that we can never have a better past so there is no point in hoping for one, much of our anger and shame is a way of holding out for God to somehow make our troubles not just go away, but never to have been. We cling to this false hope when we don't believe we can truly be happy (saved, good, loved, or whatever other positive adjective seems to be eluding us at the time) unless whatever we think is missing in our life is somehow gone back to and redone.

We can feel ashamed about having a past full of deficits and holes we cannot make disappear. We may unconsciously wonder if we have the right to live and thrive in the face of such problems. Do we have the right to take our life seriously, to have hope, to succeed, to be joyful given our history, or will we be disloyal to the realities of suffering if we mend and move on? Do we have the right to be healthy and happy when others whose lives are also flawed are not? Will God think it is okay to foist such problems upon us again if we heal and move forward?

Humility about Our History

Of all the names ascribed to Christ in holy writ, He is never called the Preventer. He is the Savior; He is the One who rescues us after the fact of our losses, not the One who keeps us out of the pit to begin with. Our losses, wounds, and broken places are not shameful testaments to our worthlessness but meeting grounds with Christ. He joins us in all of them, is forsaken with us, and eases our shame at feeling outside the bounds of normal human experience. If He—born in a manger, scorned as illegitimate, rejected, beaten, crucified—if *He* has the right to take His life seriously, to claim joy, to insist on meaning, so do we.

Our life does not have to be spectacular, important to others, or even productive to be precious. My sweet mother, afflicted with Alzheimer's, no longer can teach a lesson, keep track of birthdays, or even prepare a simple meal. But she finds joy in the beauty of the mountains, delights in the antics of her dog, and keeps alive the stories of her life's lessons. She doesn't know what year it is or what state she lives in, but she knows in whom she trusts, is grateful for blessings, and reminds me daily that life is a treasure here, now, even if here and now is all we have.

DISTINGUISHING BETWEEN SHAME AND HUMILITY

As we learn to tune out mocking voices from the great and spacious building, shame takes less of a toll on our heart. In the true humility that is the antithesis of shame, godly sorrow and divine discontent are welcome messengers instead of pointing fingers. We are more apt to repent, submit to the consequences of our choices, learn the joy of our redemption, and become less likely to run and hide from the loving face of God. We can afford the risks of growth and learning that help turn weakness to strength.

A researcher asked a classroom full of kindergarten students,

"Who in here can draw?" All hands went up enthusiastically. "Who can dance?" Demonstrations of five-year-old dance talent popped up all over the room. "Who can sing?" Enthusiastic choruses erupted. The researcher went to a college classroom and asked the same questions. One or two people timidly answered yes to each question. What happened between kindergarten and college that changed our self-definitions about what we are capable of? Did we really learn humility? Or did we mostly learn shame?

As I think about people who brought great goodness out of a wound or a weakness, what stands out is their genuine humility without shame. They work hard to heal the emotional and spiritual wounds they confront, but once that healing occurs, their scars don't stop them from showing their faces. They are modest, but they do not sit on their hands when asked to step forward and contribute. They invite others close, openly revealing their scars in testimony of the healing power of God, following the example of the Savior. If we want to turn weakness to strength, shame is not the right path.

The differences between shame or humiliation and genuine humility are summarized in the following chart.

Christ taught us to "be ye therefore perfect, even as your Father which is in heaven is perfect" (Matthew 5:48). Perfection implies two things. First is freedom from sin. Once we understand the difference between sin and weakness, freedom from sin appears to actually be possible through the Atonement of Christ, contingent on our repentance. The second implication of the word "perfect" is wholeness or completeness. This implies more than the absence of sin; it implies the acquisition of virtue. Humility in the face of our weakness is the fountainhead of these virtues. Humility includes being meek, honest, teachable, patient, and reliant on the Lord, without defensiveness or shame.

Paul testifies of Christ's absolute empathy for our weakness,

SHAME	HUMILITY
Feelings of embarrassment, worthlessness	Feelings of calm assurance
Impulse to hide weaknesses from others	Impulse to acknowledge weaknesses to others
Fear of being exposed	Self-acceptance, warts and all
Shifting responsibility and blaming others	Taking responsibility, desire to improve
Avoiding risk-taking out of fear of failure	Taking risks so as to grow and contribute
Comparing self to others who are seen as superior	Seeing weakness as common to all people
Defensive and stubborn or wishy-washy	Meek and teachable
Sarcasm or excessive seriousness	Humor and enjoyment of life and others
Preoccupation with flaws	Flaws seen in perspective
Fear of God's disapproval	Confident in God's love

Diagram 9: Shame or Humility

inviting us to come to Him boldly (confidently, unashamedly) to obtain His grace. His witness epitomizes the message of this chapter: "For we have not an high priest which cannot be touched with the feeling of our infirmities; but was in all points tempted like as we are, yet without sin. Let us therefore come boldly unto the throne of grace, that we may obtain mercy, and find grace to help in time of need" (Hebrews 4:15–16).

Chapter 6

WHEN I AM WEAK, THEN AM I STRONG

My husband, Dave, has long remembered a high priests class he once attended while visiting Jerusalem. The lesson was on the importance of the scriptures. The teacher, a convert from a humble background, asked if anyone had succeeded in reading the Book of Mormon all the way through. In the class were a number of visiting professors from Brigham Young University who had spent their entire professional lives studying holy writ. My husband felt a little embarrassed for the teacher, who didn't seem to realize who his students were. Dave could almost read the minds of the class members as they settled into the assumption that they were probably not going to learn a lot in high priests class that day. There may have even been a little smugness in the group at having so excelled in their reading duties.

The teacher was wide-eyed as all the hands in the room went up in answer to his question. He could hardly comprehend that everyone in the room had read and reread a book that he found too difficult to finish at all. But then he began to share how he tried, nevertheless, to live the principles the scriptures teach. He humbly enumerated many ways he spent time with his family—hours spent helping his children, attending their events, playing with them, counseling with them, teaching them, and showing interest in their lives. He shared many personal examples of his involvement with each child. He expressed his love and deep commitment to them. The esteemed professors got quiet. They realized humbly that there are many ways to bring the scriptures to life in our lives. Their teacher, in his humility about his weakness, taught them from great strengths.

This chapter takes us to the right side of diagram 3—the side that illustrates responding to our weakness with humility, qualifying to receive the grace that turns our weakness to strength (see page 9). These transformative gifts are accomplished through God's grace.

THE WORKINGS OF GRACE

In response to our humility about our weakness, God offers to "make weak things become strong" unto us (Ether 12:27). There must be ways for weak things to become strong other than through noticeable improvement in our ability. The high priests teacher did not turn into an expert in ancient languages or a virtuoso at scripture chase just because he was humble. Yet he became a powerful teacher to learned men who could have easily trumped him in these skills.

The Bible Dictionary defines *grace* as an "enabling power" to do what we cannot do on our own.[1] God's gift of grace fits our need precisely: when we are weak, He offers power. While we often assume this means God will turn our chicken scratches into Shakespearean sonnets, the following is noteworthy: God didn't change Moroni's writing skill (the weakness Moroni fretted over) in any observable way. Despite the promise in Ether 12:27, Moroni's writing seems to be of exactly the same quality after this promise as before. What might God have in mind when He promises that His grace will make weak things become strong unto us?

Let's consider a weakness such as laziness, which could emerge out of either physical limits on our energy or emotional limits in our work ethic. How could God make this weakness become strong? I can think of several possibilities:

1. *Eliminate the weakness.* God's grace could enable us to overcome a weakness completely. He could give us tremendous energy and a strong work ethic so we are not lazy anymore. This is what we wish for, but generally not what happens. Only occasionally will procrastinators become first movers, heavy people forever thin, or shy people party animals. How else might God turn weakness to strength?

2. *Grow into strength.* Grace could help us grow and improve in skill. For example, God could help us learn to manage our time better and learn the skills and attitudes of self-discipline to gradually improve on our laziness problem. While we are still predisposed to be lazy, we learn to combat it successfully at least much of the time by setting goals, enjoying the work we do, or breaking big tasks into small ones. This is a real and valuable possibility for turning weakness to strength, but there are others.

3. *See both sides of the coin.* Grace could help us learn to magnify the "good" aspects of a certain quality while minimizing the "bad." We could learn to enjoy our leisure and relaxation time but not opt for such "laziness" when we have a big project due at work. This option acknowledges that laziness is not just a fault; it also has its appropriate place in our lives. There is an appropriate and legitimate time for being lazy! But grace may help us not make *all* the time "lazy time."

4. *Develop compensating strengths.* Grace could help us develop

compensating strengths, like learning to work really hard in short bursts to make up for our laziness or learning to be a great listener because we are not as busily at work as others. So our lack of energy and stamina might lead us to develop other skills of genuine worth, even if we are still lazy.

5. *Acquire virtues through humility.* As we are truly humble about our laziness or other weaknesses, God may teach us to be more compassionate about the laziness in others and about their other weaknesses as well. In a similar vein, He may help us be less judgmental, more forgiving, less critical, more charitable, less competitive, more reliant on Him, and less reliant on man—all of which are strengths or virtues of exceptional value to our souls. Such virtues come through humility, regardless of what specific weakness we need to be humble about. Might these be the strengths God is most interested in endowing us with through our weakness?

6. *Participate in God's generosity.* Finally, God may simply compensate for our weakness with His Spirit and power, like testifying to others that our message is true even when we didn't get around to writing our sacrament meeting talk until that morning because we were being lazy. This is where I am most in awe of God's gracious and merciful kindness to me in my weakness.

Let's look at these six possibilities more closely.

ELIMINATE THE WEAKNESS

Many converts have had the experience of handing their cigarettes over to the missionaries and never picking them up again. When we see a habit or behavior as not just weakness but something that interferes with our access to God's Spirit, we may succeed at eliminating the previous pattern completely and immediately. God will help us eliminate weakness that includes elements of sin or rebellion against Him. When we repent and desire to obey, we can receive great spiritual strength.

Relatively few of our weaknesses fall into this category, however. We can quit smoking, for example, but we can't just quit feeling. Feelings like sadness, fear, boredom, guilt, and longing have an important role in our lives, even if they sometimes cause us problems. In fact, people who have lost their capacity for feelings due to brain damage can still learn all kinds of information but cannot make good decisions that require judgment and motivation. They struggle to function in everyday life. Eliminating our feelings would not benefit us. Instead our task is to tutor and bridle our feelings so that they are our servants, not our masters.

We also can't just quit being susceptible to temptation. Even the Savior was tempted, and given the ubiquitous presence of evil in the universe, it appears we will always have the choice to follow Satan. We do not become more like God because we lose our capacity to be tempted but because we strengthen our capacity to ignore temptation, choose truth, and delight in righteousness.

Nor can we just quit getting tired or sick. We can often choose our attitude and approach to illness, but we cannot always choose to be well. Nor does God always heal us. Sometimes illness is our passageway home; sometimes it is the trial that teaches us or others; sometimes it is the vehicle for demonstrating God's power; and sometimes it just *is* with no real meaning attached. Being ill is not a sign of failure. It may be a problem to be solved, an obstacle to be worked around, a pattern that may yield to time and patience, or a fate to be lived with gracefully if nothing else works.

Similarly, mental illnesses such as depression, anxiety, personality disorders, and so on cannot generally just be eliminated at will. As with other illnesses, God does not always heal us even when we have faith, obey His laws, and desire it. Sometimes such illnesses emerge from characteristics of our physical bodies and sometimes they are highly influenced by our past experience or present circumstances. Our personal righteousness is not a guarantee of immunity to these things, any more than righteousness always spares us from physical illness. The Lord's counsel is, "And whosoever among you are sick, and have not faith to be healed, but believe, shall be nourished with all tenderness . . . and that not by the hand of an enemy" (D&C 42:43). Mental illness, like any other illness, can tutor us in many virtues and bless many people, but sometimes we have to take a very long view to appreciate these potential strengths.

When we must deal with a weakness such as same-sex attraction, addiction, or difficulty with impulse control, we may or may not eliminate the weakness even if we do not indulge in sinful behavior. Our desire can be firm to obey God and keep His commandments, but we may continue to notice temptations, longings, or persistent ideas that reflect the patterns of our human weakness. We may wonder if our hearts are in the right place because we continue to be tempted or to struggle. I firmly believe that God is empathic, patient, and understanding with such human weakness. There is a big difference between being tempted (which happens to all of us) and courting temptation. We avoid courting temptation both by steering clear of certain places and people and by fortifying ourselves with adequate sleep and nutrition, scripture study and prayer, good friends, and good stress management skills.

I well remember a seminar I once attended on sexual addiction. The instructor was a sex addict who was successfully staying "sober." A participant asked, "So do you just get stronger and stronger at resisting temptation, or do you actually get to a point where you are no longer tempted?"

I appreciated the instructor's thoughtful reply. He said in essence, "I am no longer tempted as much because I stay away from temptation, but when temptation comes anyway, which it does, I don't engage it. Instead of staying in the temptation and resisting it, I move away from the scene of battle. I call friends and get involved in constructive activities. I get a good night's sleep. I find a funny movie. I do yoga. I think about why I'm feeling lonely or overwhelmed, and I make changes. I'm still tempted sometimes, but my responses to the temptation have changed. Now I know how to reduce the temptation and deal with my underlying problem instead of fighting the temptation in ignorant solitude. Temptation is no longer a cue to act out. Now it is a cue to take better care of myself and meet my real needs."

As we have previously noted, the Savior invites, "Wherefore, *settle* this in your hearts, that ye will do the things which I shall teach, and command you" (JST Luke 14:28; emphasis added). Sometimes it is enough to truly settle a matter in our hearts for our behavior to follow. This does not mean settling in my heart that I will just have to increase my tolerance for being frustrated or disappointed. Rather, it means settling in my heart that God is good and will not invite me to do things unless they will greatly bless me, even if I cannot in the moment understand how. When I cultivate this truth deeply, I don't have to keep making the same decision over and over.

Consider: What previous weaknesses have you overcome or virtually eliminated? How did you start? How did you sustain it? What did you learn? How do you handle it when the desire to indulge comes back? Reflecting on these questions may help you discover principles that will help you approach other weaknesses more successfully as well.

GROW INTO STRENGTH

When God promises to make weak things strong in us, I don't think he is promising to make one thing into something completely unrelated, like apple seeds into steel girders. Instead he is promising to make weak things into the strong version of the weak thing, like apple seeds into a strong tree. Many of our most important strengths grow out of the seeds of weakness in one way or another. The puny, crushable seed and the strong, vibrant tree are not different in their essence, only in their stage of development. The mighty tree emerges when the right conditions are provided to foster the seed's growth.

In a similar way, when God says He will make weak things become strong He is reminding us that weakness and strength are often inherently alike. Our job is not to transform weakness into something completely different but to create the conditions conducive to growth from the first state to the second. Those conditions include humility and faith. Humility implies making effort, being teachable, getting help, exercising patience, and prioritizing. Faith reminds us of our reliance on the Lord and our trust in His capacity to bless us. Whether we are learning the piano, developing a sense of humor, growing a savings account, becoming kinder, or trying to exercise regularly, growth and improvement mean seeing our mistakes, trusting the Lord, and continuing to try and learn.

In Greek mythology, the gods punished Sisyphus for trickery and deceitfulness by condemning him to push a huge boulder up a mountain. As he approached the mountaintop, the boulder would roll back down to the bottom and Sisyphus would have to start over. Sisyphus has become the symbol of frustrating, pointless tasks that must be done over and over again (which is how exercise or practicing music scales feels to me). But what if, as a sacrament meeting speaker I once heard proposed, Sisyphus did not see his task as getting the boulder to the top of the mountain? What if he saw his task as training for the Olympics, building strength and endurance to fulfill his gold-medal dream? Then, instead of seeing his task as pointless and frustrating, he would see rolling the boulder up the mountain again and again as valuable and productive.

If we feel that our weaknesses are only boulders we must push again and again, never succeeding at getting them where they are supposed to go, then our weaknesses will be a source of constant frustration and discouragement. We may wonder if we can endure a lifetime of struggle against the gravity of our personal mountain. But if we see our weakness as our personalized version of the muscle-building boulder of Sisyphus and ourselves as future spiritual Olympians, then we can approach our challenge differently.

Consider: What is a skill or talent you have now? What was it like when you first began to develop it? What did it take to improve? How might these principles apply to a weakness you are currently developing into a strength?

SEE BOTH SIDES OF THE COIN

Sometimes strengths and weaknesses are flip sides of the same coin: What appears as weakness in one context may be strength in another context or from another perspective. I demonstrate this principle in counseling by asking married individuals two questions. First, "What attracted you to your (future) spouse?" Then, "What about your spouse is driving you crazy these days?"

With amazing frequency, answers to these two questions will be closely related. The person who was drawn to a spouse who is warm and affectionate will end up feeling smothered or threatened by all that "neediness." The person who was impressed with the spouse's work ethic becomes annoyed that the spouse is so consumed by a career. The person who delighted in a spouse's spontaneity becomes frustrated that nothing can be planned ahead. The person who once felt safe and secure with a spouse who is steady and frugal ends up criticizing the spouse as boring and stingy. The list goes on.

Many of our character traits are not unilateral strengths or weaknesses but qualities that have potential for either good or ill depending on timing, balance, frequency, and pervasiveness. As we see our traits and patterns from this broader perspective we can feel less shame about the weakness side of the coin. We can work instead to be more tactful in using our skills, better at balancing them with other important qualities, more humble and teachable as we recognize their impact on others, and more flexible in our repertoire of responses to a given situation. We can also recognize that other people also hold two-sided coins which we can view with more tolerance and kindness.

Consider: What is a weakness you have that concerns you? What strengths might be on the flip side of that coin? If you don't know, ask someone who knows you well to help you see these strengths.

DEVELOP COMPENSATING STRENGTHS

Someone recently e-mailed me a link to a video of a South American man with no arms who could play the guitar with his toes. I've also seen clips of a man born blind who was a talented artist, a gifted yoga teacher in a wheelchair, a man with no arms who called himself a "hugging machine," and a concert pianist with only two fingers on each hand. While such accomplishments amaze me, each of us in one way or another can develop strengths to compensate for our weaknesses—strengths that allow us to succeed in unlikely places and against the odds.

What would we do as a church without people who are too

nervous to teach but who happily work in the library, people who never sign up to make casseroles but are always there to clean the building, people who don't have dramatic spiritual experiences but believe the testimony of others, people who aren't very good at controlling their anger but have mastered the art of effective apologies, people with annoying personal traits who pay full tithes and always drive the welfare truck? In Zion there are no poor. In other words, there is no one with nothing to give.

Perhaps the single most helpful tool I've learned when struggling with my weaknesses is to ask myself what I have to gain from my weaknesses and not just what I stand to lose. In this simple change of viewpoint, new worlds of possibility can open. A stellar example of this principle is found in one of my favorite books, *And There Was Light*, written by Jacques Lusseyran, a Frenchman who became completely blind after a childhood accident. He writes vividly of what he stood to gain from his blindness amid all that he had lost. So vividly, in fact, that I found myself envious of his gifts.

Lusseyran became a leader in the French Resistance during World War II and survived the concentration camps by living out of these gifts. He writes of his journey from frustration over his weakness to comfort and delight in his newfound gifts:

"In the days immediately after the operation ... I still wanted to use my eyes. I followed their usual path. I looked in the direction where I was in the habit of seeing before the accident, and there was anguish, a lack, something like a void which filled me with what grownups call despair.

"Finally, one day, and it was not long in coming, I realized that I was looking in the wrong way. . . .

". . . I began to look more closely, not at things but at a world closer to myself, looking from an inner place to one further within, instead of clinging to the movement of sight toward the world outside.

"Immediately, the substance of the universe drew together, redefined and peopled itself anew. I was aware of a radiance emanating from a place I knew nothing about, a place which might as well have been outside me as within. But radiance was there, or, to put it more precisely, light. . . .

" . . . I bathed in it as an element which blindness had suddenly brought much closer. . . .

" . . . at every waking hour and even in my dreams I lived in a stream of light."[2]

I read Lusseyran's description and can't help but feel that his blindness opened up something to him that I long to see—the pervasive and very real light of Christ. He learned to cultivate this light through attitudes of trust, confidence, and caring. He explains:

"Still, there were times when the light faded, almost to the point of disappearing. It happened every time I was afraid.

" . . . What the loss of my eyes had not accomplished was brought about by fear. It made me blind.

"Anger and impatience had the same effect, throwing everything into confusion. . . .

"When I was playing with my small companions, if I suddenly grew anxious to win, to be first at all costs, then all at once I could see nothing. Literally I went into fog or smoke.

" . . . But when I was happy and serene, approached people with confidence and thought well of them, I was rewarded with light. . . .

"Armed with such a tool, why should I need a moral code? For me this tool took the place of red and green lights. I always knew where the road was open and where it was closed. I had only to look at the bright signal which taught me how to live."[3]

I come away from Lusseyran's autobiography convinced that for every loss inherent in the mortal experience, doors can open to new realities and gifts we could not otherwise "see."

Consider: Your weaknesses have closed some doors for you, but perhaps others have opened. What do you stand to gain as you accept your weaknesses and work with them instead of against them? What gifts have come from your difficulties or challenges?

ACQUIRE VIRTUES THROUGH HUMILITY

Lusseyran's story reminds me that one of the most important uses of weakness is to fit me for the kingdom of God. Weakness is the great equalizer, the human trait we all share.

Our specific weaknesses differ, but just as "all have sinned, and come short of the glory of God" (Romans 3:23), we all are weak and fall short of our righteous desires. Yet God gives us weakness and for a specific cause: that we might be humble. Through humility we can learn the essential traits of charity, forgiveness, compassion, patience, courage, temperance, diligence, resilience, and hope. One could write whole books on the value of each of these qualities. We may never overcome all our weaknesses in this life, but these sweet strengths are far more influential in our eternal progression than our weaknesses.

Ether 12:37 clarifies exactly how God intends to make Moroni's particular weakness into a strength. It is not by eliminating his weakness, changing it into something else, looking on the bright side of it, or showing him the gifts that might compensate for it, as promising as these possibilities are for many things. Rather, God says: "Thou hast been faithful; wherefore, thy garments shall be made clean. And because thou hast seen thy weakness *thou shalt be made strong, even unto the sitting down in the place which I have prepared in the mansions of my Father*" (Ether 12:37; emphasis added).

The humility that can emerge from seeing our weakness fosters the very virtues that fit us to sit down with God. In particular, humility about our weakness can teach us charity, the strength Moroni declares is essential to eternal life with God: "Except men shall have charity they cannot inherit that place which thou hast prepared in the mansions of thy Father" (Ether 12:34).

A man I'll call Kenny had a very difficult mission and did not get along well with his mission president. This was a source of pain and deep disappointment in his life. Some years later Kenny served in a bishopric that conducted a disciplinary council for a young woman who had also had a troubled relationship with her mission president. Upon coming home from her mission she committed a moral transgression, blaming her behavior on her deeply unsatisfying mission experience. Kenny not only felt and communicated great empathy for this sister but was able to counsel her constructively about other ways to approach her frustration, the importance of repentance, and the need to forgive. Both Kenny and the young sister found healing and support in this shared experience. The sister found strength to repent and return to the Church, in part because she experienced Kenny as a Church leader whose empathy was genuine and personal. And Kenny found a depth of charity he might not otherwise have felt as a result of humbly allowing the Lord to use his painful past to bless another. For the first time since his own mission, Kenny was able to use his experience for good.

Consider: What character strengths have you acquired through struggling against your human weakness?

PARTICIPATE IN GOD'S GENEROSITY

A final way God turns our weakness into strength is also implied in Ether 12:26. Here God tells Moroni that even though some of the Gentiles will mock his weakness in writing, God's grace will be sufficient for those who are meek. In other words, God promises to simply compensate for Moroni's weakness out of His strength, even though Moroni's weak writing would not normally produce the desired result.

We don't especially want our children to know about this option; we want them to accept that they have to work hard to improve or they will never get what they want. But ultimately God did not wait for Moroni to get his graduate degree in literature to intervene in his dilemma. God compensated for Moroni's weakness in writing by promising His Spirit to others rather than by changing Moroni's skill with words. To be sure, Moroni was doing his best as well, but the point is that Moroni had a weakness he did not overcome in any demonstrable way. God simply worked around it. And in doing so He teaches us all to depend on *His* mighty arm—not on Moroni's, not on our own.

More often than we like to admit, this is the case for each of us. I still believe God expects us to work hard to learn, grow, and contribute. But because we are weak, we will simply never be able to accomplish by our own effort all the things that are needed. We will always have weaknesses that we have not prioritized just yet because we are limited and insufficient in ourselves. We will give many things less than our best shot. We will simply not know how to accomplish all we would like to do. We will be imperfect and inadequate at managing our emotions, responding to temptation, coping with our illnesses and hurts, overcoming pride and shame, developing our skills, magnifying our callings, managing our time, and learning from our mistakes. Yet God in His infinite kindness will often compensate for our weakness out of His great generosity, even when we have not done our best or given our all in our own judgment.

I don't offer this as an excuse for slacking off but as a simple observation from my own life. I do believe God expects us to do our part, to try, to work hard, and to step up to the plate. But it is also my experience that He is incredibly generous and patient when we are dealing with genuine weakness. On more than one occasion when I felt I did not deserve it, He has stepped in anyway and made my less-than-best effort or less-than-smartest decision or less-than-noblest motivation work, compensating for my weakness with His strength.

These are the moments when my gratitude and humility and wonder at His goodness are almost boundless and inevitably bring me to tears. I hope I never take such moments for granted or assume they are my due. I also hope I don't use such moments to beat myself up for my limitations, even though my limitations are real. Rather I hope such experiences will prompt my deepest gratitude and deepen my sense of being held and sustained by His tender and compassionate care. He loves us. He knows us. His goodness is truly infinite.

Consider: When has God compensated for your weakness despite your inadequacy? How can you remember this blessing and allow it to deepen your awareness of God's goodness and love for you?

WEAK *AND* STRONG

Paul reports this conversation—this hopeful conversation—with God: "And he said unto me, My grace is sufficient for thee: for my strength is made perfect in weakness. Most gladly therefore will I rather glory in my infirmities, that the power of Christ may rest upon me. Therefore I take pleasure in infirmities, in reproaches, in necessities, in persecutions, in distresses for Christ's sake: for when I am weak, then am I strong" (2 Corinthians 12:9–10).

Elder Neal A. Maxwell, contemplating what we can do to manage our "vexing feelings of inadequacy," suggests: "We can make quiet but more honest inventories of our strengths. Most of us are dishonest bookkeepers and need confirming 'outside auditors.' He who in the first estate was thrust down delights in having us put ourselves down. Self-contempt is of Satan; there is none of it in heaven. We should, of course, learn from our mistakes, but without forever viewing the instant replays lest these become the game of life itself."[4]

In the end, God can turn mortal weakness to strength in a variety of ways. Our task is to learn from weakness, see it in context, stop Satan from using it to lead us into sin, and allow God to use our weakness to build our character and our love for Him instead. This doesn't mean that we allow weakness free rein or that weakness doesn't also create problems for us and others. It just means that weakness is not only *not* sin but a potential source of blessings. Among the greatest of these blessings is the opportunity to feel and know God's amazing and compassionate kindness to us, His weak but cherished children.

Chapter 7

LIVING FROM STRENGTHS

My father recently passed away after a long and debilitating illness. He was a World War II and commercial pilot who still flew a private plane at eighty, golfed and skied well into his seventies, and only gave up driving his Corvette a few months before his death at age eighty-five. He and I had our last argument over politics the day before his death, and the number of magazines and stock market newsletters he read regularly overflows my mailbox months later. As he neared the end of his life, he spent most of his time sleeping in a recliner, had lost all feeling in his hands and legs, and could get around only in a motorized scooter. He fought valiantly for every bit of independence he could cling to, although his independence took him to the absolute limits of his endurance. In fact, the effort expended simply to get dressed by himself was ultimately too much for his heart, and he died in the attempt.

Meanwhile, my mother faces the long, slow decline associated with Alzheimer's disease. She walks her dog every day, loves shopping for new clothes, and flirts with my husband like a high school girl. But she has no idea what the dog's name is, can't figure out who the clothes belong to once she gets them home, and doesn't always remember that her own husband is gone. She can't track a television show or a book, can't fix herself a meal, can't participate in a Sunday School class, can't remember how old she is or where she lives. She has become a caricature of her own best and worst traits, and she will never get any better. Yet she prays with feeling, tears up at a spiritual story, and loves the Lord.

WHAT MAKES LIFE WORTH LIVING?

As I have watched my parents face the physical and intellectual declines that come with aging, the question of what makes life worth living sometimes haunts me. What makes life sweet even in the face of enormous obstacles? What makes life pointless even when we have every comfort? What gives meaning to life even when it is marred by great suffering? Is life worth living if we cannot take care of ourselves any longer, do the things we used to love, remember the children we bore, or serve the country we risked our lives for? For that matter, do my daily routines, my struggles against obstacles, my efforts to love or sacrifice, my thoughtfulness or personal growth—do any of these things matter given my ultimate demise?

The gospel of Jesus Christ affirms that in all life's circumstances and changes, we declare with our choices what we truly love. Reiterating the model on which this book is based, we declare that we choose God when we repent of our sins and bring our weaknesses to Him to turn to strengths. Just as importantly, we choose Him by what we choose to tend and make grow among our opportunities and strengths. We both learn vital lessons and contribute to the world through these processes. In doing so, we accomplish our personal missions and we can find joy. Joy is a legitimate answer to our questions about what makes life worth living: we are that we might have joy (see 2 Nephi 2:25).

Joy is more than momentary pleasure in favorable circumstances. Experience teaches us that we can find joy even in the midst of suffering and that great joy often comes through enduring hardship, not just from eliminating it. We can find joy in sacrificing momentary well-being in pursuit of a valued goal or in service to someone we love. Joy abounds in character, not just convenience. My father, who did not believe in an afterlife, found life meaningful only if joy could be achieved here and now, so he spent his final days in misery. But the promises of eternity bring my mother much peace despite earth's losses and difficulties. What brings us joy and how we pursue it expresses what we love and value for its own sake. Hope and trust in Christ are sufficient to bring us peace and joy in our redemption even when earthly happiness eludes us. Happiness that is grounded in righteous living deepens into joy.

Some good people have a quiet sense of joy that permeates much of daily life. Other good people experience joy as an epiphany of feeling that is rare but of great worth. Still other good people struggle with depression or circumstances that make feeling joy elusive, but their trust in the promise of joy can still be strong. Current research suggests that about 50 percent of the variability in human happiness comes wired into our genes—some people are just born with a proclivity for happiness. Another 10 percent of our happiness varies with our circumstances—where we live and with whom, how much money we make, the work we do, the weather we put up with. The remaining 40 percent of our happiness is within our control; it is something we can cultivate or ignore.[1] Even if we come into this life with a predisposition to depression, even if our circumstances are meager, we can cultivate attitudes, skills, and a trusting connection with God that foster meaning and joy.

When we repent of our sins, bring our weaknesses to God in humility, exercise our faith and hope in Christ, and build a life of contribution from our strengths, we are enough, even if our lives are not amazing by any earthly standard. We are enough even though we are weak; we are enough even if our talents are meager; we are enough even if we lose much of what has formerly given us a sense of identity and purpose. We are enough, and joy is our due, whether in this life or in the next. This hope brings meaning and purpose to even our most difficult days.

The gospel suggests many sources of joy. Scriptural accounts record people finding great joy through

+ experiencing God's astounding goodness and love for His children (see Alma 26:16, 35, 37).
+ bringing others to God (see Alma 26:30; D&C 18:16).
+ fasting, praying, and keeping the Sabbath day holy (see Helaman 3:35; D&C 59:10).
+ repenting and receiving God's mercy (see Mosiah 4:3; Alma 36:20–21).
+ seeing the fruit of one's righteous labors (see Jacob 5:60).
+ accomplishing one's mission and callings on earth (see Alma 29:13).
+ helping others succeed in their callings (see Alma 29:14, 16).
+ communing with God and receiving answers to prayer (see John 16:24; Alma 29:10).
+ learning spiritual truths (see 1 John 1:1–4).
+ seeing loved ones happy and safe (see 1 Nephi 5:7; Alma 56:56).
+ sharing profound spiritual experiences with others (see Helaman 6:3; 3 Nephi 17:17–20).

God's plan for His children is called the plan of happiness (see Alma 42:8), and happiness and joy seem to be the ultimate expression of the good life, the life worth living. So how do we cultivate them? Psychologist Martin Seligman proposes that happiness is a by-product of a balance of three categories of activities. Any of them can lead us to happiness, but the third category seems especially relevant for joy. The categories are as follows:

+ Pleasurable activities (like enjoying good food or a lovely sunset—things that please the senses).
+ Engaging activities (like tackling a big work project— things that interest and involve us to the point that we get lost in them).
+ Meaningful activities (like helping a friend or praying with feeling—things that reflect our deepest values and connect us with something bigger than ourselves).[2]

Developing and using our strengths (character virtues like authenticity, courage, generosity, self-control, and gratitude) play a major role in all three types of activities. Strengths like appreciation of beauty and gratitude for life's goodness help my mother delight in the grandeur of the mountains and the smiles of children even if she cannot remember their names. Strengths like perseverance, bravery, and love of learning kept my dad engaged in life even when his body was failing. Strengths like his loyalty to country or her faith in religious convictions have brought meaning and purpose to both my parents, even through great personal challenges. Living out of our strengths is invigorating and sustaining. It puts us in touch with our most authentic self. And it is a consistent road to happiness and joy.

IDENTIFYING STRENGTHS

If we want to live out of our strengths, it helps to know what they are.

I spend a fair amount of time fretting about my weaknesses. One day I decided to read my patriarchal blessing to look for my weaknesses so I would be sure not to miss any. To my surprise, I could count them on one hand, and even that required a pretty liberal interpretation of "weakness." (For example, my blessing urges me to be humble, so I assumed one of my weaknesses was pride.) Then I decided to count the strengths—the virtues, gifts, talents, blessings, and opportunities enumerated in my blessing. I found fifty-two. It seems that even though God gives us weakness, He is far more generous with strengths. Strengths may include or evolve out of the following:

- Virtues such as wisdom, spirituality, courage, love, temperance, or justice
- Spiritual gifts, such as faith, charity, wisdom, revelation, or healing
- Talents, such as music, art, athleticism, intelligence, or sense of direction
- Skills we develop, such as reading, gardening, computer literacy, yoga, or quilting
- Blessings, such as children, health, prosperity, employment, or nature
- Opportunities, such as callings, projects, relationships, travel, or competitions

A current movement in the field of psychology supports the idea that happiness and meaning are not found primarily in overcoming our faults but in using our strengths. We may feel relief when we work on reducing a weakness; we may feel noble when we exhibit a character virtue that does not come easily to us; but we feel alive, happy, engaged, and enriched when we use our strengths.

To be sure, when we really have significant personality flaws or character deficits, we would be well served to devote energy to bringing such weaknesses to at least "neutral." But the goal of life is not to obsess over our flaws at the expense of exploring our gifts. When most of our energy every day is spent expressing and developing our genuine and God-given strengths, virtues, righteous desires, and spiritual gifts, we become happier and life takes on rich meaning. It is tedious and discouraging to spend every day preoccupied with our weaknesses.

Even when we are ill or in pain, even when we have serious problems, even when the work we have to do is boring and repetitive, and even when we are combating challenges, we long for meaning and purpose. We want to know that our problems do not define us. We want to know that we can still contribute. Blessedly, we don't have to wait for a cure for our cancer or a fix for our struggling marriage in order to start developing our virtues and spiritual gifts. In fact, developing such strengths and gifts can give us hope and courage with which to face our adversities more constructively. People don't just get happier when they overcome their problems. They overcome their problems when they become happier.

We can become more aware of our strengths in the following four ways: by looking at patriarchal blessings, by assessing our signature strengths, by examining the cues hidden in our jealousies, and by recognizing what we love.

1. *Patriarchal blessings—the search for gifts and blessings.* You might find it interesting to make a copy of your patriarchal blessing and use different colored highlighters to mark (1) weaknesses that could become strengths (temptations, "negative" emotions, illnesses, challenges, or problems that are stated or implied), and (2) spiritual gifts,

blessings, opportunities, callings, and virtues. Given the particular family constellation, work environment, church calling, or personal challenges you face at this time, what strengths and gifts are most relevant for accomplishing your current mission?

In addition to patriarchal blessings, you might consider other blessings, conversations with friends and family members, and personal spiritual promptings that allude to your spiritual gifts and opportunities. Some of these gifts and blessings may especially resonate for you now. These deserve your attention and investment.

2. *Signature strengths—the search for character and virtue.* Martin Seligman, founder of positive psychology and former president of the American Psychological Association, is a professed agnostic. Nevertheless, he and his colleagues looked to the great religions of humankind to find the keys to good character and a happy life. They identified twenty-four signature strengths that virtually every major religious tradition or philosophy over thousands of years has seen as essential to good character.

Our signature strengths refer to what we love and value, not just what we do well, so they say something important about us. We may admire people's talents, but we admire the people themselves who exhibit character. Signature strengths like perseverance, courage, love of learning, or hope help us develop a talent and use it for good.

The twenty-four signature strengths are grouped under six major virtues[3]—qualities we see extolled in the scriptures again and again. As you read through this list, select two or three traits that you especially value and that you are known for by others:

Wisdom and knowledge—cognitive strengths in acquiring and using knowledge

- Curiosity—appreciating novelty, ambiguity, and the uncommon; inquisitive

+ Love of learning—enjoying reading and experiences that enhance knowledge
+ Open-mindedness—looking at all sides of an issue; critical thinking skills
+ Creativity—thinking about things in new ways; ingenuity in problem solving
+ Perspective—ability to see the big picture; objectivity

Courage—emotional strength of accomplishing goals in the face of opposition

+ Bravery—facing physical or social danger despite fear; taking difficult stands
+ Perseverance—finishing what one starts without getting sidetracked
+ Authenticity—keeping one's word; being honest and genuine
+ Zest—throwing oneself into life; having zeal and passion about one's activities

Temperance—emotional strengths that protect against excesses

+ Self-regulation—controlling one's emotions and behaviors; self-disciplined
+ Prudence—exercising caution; resisting impulses that impede long-term goals
+ Forgiveness—giving others a second chance; letting go of revenge
+ Modesty—unpretentiousness; downplaying one's own importance

Humanity—interpersonal strengths that provide closeness and care for others

+ Kindness and generosity—caring for others; empathy; volunteering; a desire to help

+ Social intelligence—fitting in with others; awareness of others' feelings
+ Loving and accepting love—valuing closeness; ability to both give and receive love

Justice—interpersonal strengths that support healthy communities
+ Teamwork—loyalty; citizenship; a sense of duty and commitment to the group
+ Fairness—treating others equally even if they are different or disadvantaged
+ Leadership—organizing and motivating others while maintaining good relationships

Transcendence—spiritual strengths that connect us to the universe and provide meaning
+ Appreciation of beauty and excellence—delight in nature, art, skill, or excellence
+ Gratitude—counting one's blessings; expressing thanks; delighting in life's goodness
+ Hope—expecting good outcomes and a positive future based on effort today
+ Humor and playfulness—ability to have fun, play, joke, and make others smile
+ Religiousness—a strong belief system; feeling connected to God

You may have a pretty good idea of which traits you most value or exhibit. If you want a more scientific accounting go to www.authentichappiness.org and take the *VIA Signatures Strengths Test* to identify your signature strengths compared to other people. (This research site is free and is a fun way for you and your family members to determine and compare and contrast preferred strengths.)

Using our top signature strengths is energizing, meaningful, and a source of great satisfaction and delight. In contrast, trying to express those that don't come as naturally to us can be difficult or draining, especially at first. (This doesn't mean we ignore these virtues, it just means we may not want to tackle them all at once.) We want to especially focus on expressing and developing our strengths.

3. *Analyzing our jealousies—the search for what we want and what we have.* Doctrine and Covenants 67:10 exhorts early Church leaders: "Inasmuch as you strip yourselves from jealousies and fears, and humble yourselves before me, for ye are not sufficiently humble, the veil shall be rent and you shall see me and know that I am— not with the carnal neither natural mind, but with the spiritual."

Jealousy and envy impede our spiritual progress, but sometimes dissecting our jealousies a bit can help us get back on track with our own mission and purpose. When we feel jealous of someone else's accomplishments, sometimes it is because we are neglecting our own mission and gifts. We may neglect our mission out of fear of failure, uncertainty about next steps, or distraction with lesser things. Whatever the cause, jealousy can remind us to take another look at how we are spending our energy and resources.

When I was to be released as a stake Relief Society president, my stake president asked for my thoughts about who might replace me. My thoughts immediately went to Helen, my own ward Relief Society president, a woman of great warmth whom every sister thought was her best friend. When she was in fact called as the new stake Relief Society president, she told me with considerable trepidation that she did not feel adequate to the job. I have a Ph.D. in psychology. Helen has a high school education. I am comfortable with public speaking and am a published author. Helen felt she had little to say. My husband was the bishop. Helen's husband had just joined the Church, even though she had been a member for nearly forty years.

What I saw, and what Helen did not immediately recognize, was that God did not need another Wendy as stake Relief Society president. The sisters in my stake had already had plenty of me. Those who appreciated my style had gotten their fill, and those who did not needed to know there are many ways to be a Latter-day Saint woman, many ways to be a leader, and many ways to be approved and loved by God. They did not need another crafted speech. They needed an arm around their shoulder, a warm smile and happy sense of humor, a voice of courage and hope in the face of life's challenges.

Helen wished she had my strengths. I wished, with some feelings of jealousy, for hers. Neither of us was particularly well served by our envy, except that when we realized it went both ways, we were both prompted to accept the stalemate and get back to what we each did best. Of course, we could also see and learn from what the other had that we lacked. For me, that meant giving full effort to my writing and speaking opportunities but also being a little softer, kinder, and more approachable. For Helen it meant playing to her strengths of friendliness, humor, leadership, and warmth but also letting herself grow as the great communicator she is within her own style and interests. For both of us it meant being a little more like each other but mostly more ourselves. Envy can be a cue that prompts us in the direction of what we need to focus on. And once we take the cue, envy can subside.

Envious of my neighbor's great job? Perhaps it is time to bite the bullet and go back to school. OR, remember what I love about my own job and why it works for me.

Envious of a sibling's marriage? Maybe I need to invest more in my own marriage. OR, if I'm single, it might mean I get more involved in my singles' ward and become a better visiting teacher.

Envious of a ward member's great spiritual strengths? It might be time to set aside more time for scripture study and prayer. OR, remember how much attention I give to and how positive I feel about orchestrating great family home evenings for my kids.

Envious of a superstar's good looks? Consider asking a good hair stylist or personal trainer to teach me some tricks. OR, keep working on my killer sense of humor.

A side note: some people seem to unconsciously but consistently evoke a lot of envy in others, perhaps because they have taken self-esteem from feeling slightly superior in a particular domain, or because they feel quite inadequate elsewhere. Sometimes our best approach in such relationships is to note our feeling of envy, concede the victory willingly and kindly, and make a decision not to compete.

Who do you feel competitive with? What do they have that you wish you had (or what can they do that you wish you could do)? What risks would you need to take or what would be the next step in developing your own gifts or accomplishing your own mission?

4. *What moves us—the search for what we love.* We often find our strengths and gifts in what we love—the activities we find energizing and enjoyable even when they require effort. These are the things that we can get lost in, that feel satisfying and worthwhile even if they are hard. They may be as ordinary as doing the dishes or riding a bike, or as complex as performing heart surgery or raising a challenging child, but these are the things that seem to come naturally, that we sign up for even when we know they will take time or effort, and that give us a deep sense of satisfaction. Our personal mission will often emerge from these deep interests. God calls to us through what we love.

One of the most helpful questions ever asked me was, "What

would you do with your life if you were guaranteed success?" This question helped me see more clearly what I would be willing to spend my life learning and investing in if I could have even a chance of doing it well. I was not guaranteed success of course—no one is—but the question helped me identify what I love enough to work at even if I falter at some steps along the way. I thought how foolish it would be to spend my life on things that would hurt less to fail at because I cared less about them.

Whether what we love most provides us with a living or a passionate sideline that makes life worth living, what we love, what fascinates us, what we would gladly do even if we had to pay someone else for the privilege is often the siren song by which God calls us to our life's work.

We often find a keen sense of personal mission where what we love (like organizing or learning) meets one of the world's challenges to ignite a powerful energy. My friend Nancy exemplifies this energy for me. Nancy has an unusual and highly specialized gift of spiritual sight: she sees potential. What's more, she has the gifts to bring potential to life. She goes with her husband on a mission to Africa and hates seeing abandoned children, and she soon finds herself going regularly to provide needed supplies and caring arms. She later returns to try to set up a school to help them. She looks at an older home and sees exactly how a wall might be knocked out here or a room configured there to make the house function beautifully. She looks at a stake youth program, sees undeveloped talent and confidence, and organizes a stake play or a powerful youth conference to meet the need. She sees educational needs that are not being met by current systems, and she founds a school for adolescents with learning disabilities. Nancy is one who sees things others do not and then acts.

I used to think Nancy had a very unusual gift, and in many ways

I still think that is true. But each of us has been uniquely positioned by our lives to see or hear things others might not and to act on that sure perception. Some of us can see neglect. Some hear the cry of abuse. Some of us see the delicate balance of nature. Others hear the call of the stars. Some see battles worth waging. Others hear the faintest whispers of options for peace. These gifts can prompt us to action and mobilize our finest efforts.

What do you find energizing and enjoyable that a lot of people would probably find draining and demanding? What would you do if you were guaranteed success? Which world or community problems most distress you? Which of these would you most love to impact for good?

STRENGTHS IN ACTION

As you summarize your thoughts from this self-analysis, I hope that you have noticed some trends. The gifts, virtues, talents, and righteous desires you have identified, when consciously and regularly used, can bring more meaning, purpose, and satisfaction to your life. Try brainstorming new and interesting ways that you could use your signature strengths every day for a week. In several large research studies, people who completed this exercise and used their signature strengths systematically for just a week reported an increase in happiness that lasted several months. Those who kept finding new ways to use their signature strengths after the first week experienced the greatest increase in happiness.[4]

If gospel teachings were not convincing enough, research shows that people can significantly reduce their depression or increase their sense of happiness by simply writing down each day three good things that happened and why they happened, or by writing a letter of gratitude to someone they had not properly thanked who had

had a big impact on their life, then reading the letter to that individual in person. Exercising character strengths like optimism and gratitude have a demonstrable and lasting effect on our sense of personal well-being.[5]

My husband, Dave, is a renowned thought leader in the fields of leadership and human resources. He has always been a vocal proponent of the importance of identifying and living from our strengths, not just hammering away at our weaknesses. Lately Dave has added a vital modifier to positive psychology's adage to live from our strengths: "Live from strengths *that strengthen others.*"

This suggests that we not only use our creativity but use it to tackle human problems and help other people. It means developing a sense of humor not just to be seen as witty but to brighten people's lives, ease their burdens, and help them feel good about learning. It means our perseverance is not just about finishing our work but about always being there for the people we love. It means our heart will return again and again to the question, "How can what I do well strengthen others?" Not only does this help us live a more righteous life than if we focused on our strengths alone but it helps us live a happier life. People are the ultimate meaning, and human happiness or joy is the ultimate currency in God's economy. We take our moral compass from what benefits people, bringing them long-term well-being and satisfaction.

SPIRITUAL STRENGTHS

For many Latter-day Saints, religiousness or spirituality is a signature strength. Spirituality includes a strong sense of meaning and purpose, a coherent belief system, and a personal sense of calling or mission. It includes feeling loved by God and being connected to the Spirit through prayer and inspiration. Even if no one else is around or our current lifestyle is isolating, spirituality provides connections that are deeply meaningful.

Dennis Charney, M.D., Ph.D., and head of psychiatric research at Mt. Sinai School of Medicine, studies POWs who were incarcerated for many years but who do not show the typical symptoms of post-traumatic stress disorder. Genetic predispositions to resilience and a lack of trauma in one's early life play a large role in how people deal with stress, but Charney also found that skills and choices helped many POWs to survive and thrive. These characteristics include the spiritual strengths of faith in God, a rock-solid belief system, a firm moral compass, and a sense of meaningful connection with other people.[6]

Different spiritual strengths are like different languages through which we receive and express the Spirit. Good, spiritual people may excel in some of these languages but struggle with others. Accepting that our spouses and children have different spiritual signature strengths from ours can lead to greater peace in our families. Although our native spiritual languages are the most satisfying, we can learn new spiritual languages so we can better share spiritual experiences with people we love.

Some of the spiritual languages different people cherish include the following:

+ Prayer
+ Service or helping others
+ Scripture study
+ Sacred music
+ Church attendance
+ Visiting sacred sites
+ Temple work

+ Meditating (perhaps while sewing, driving, walking, or gardening)
+ Missionary work
+ Being in nature
+ Researching or writing family history
+ Sharing testimonies
+ Teaching or speaking
+ Caring for children, the aged, or the sick
+ Keeping a journal or scrapbook
+ Planning spiritual events for others
+ Reading spiritually focused books
+ Planning meetings
+ Counseling with others
+ Fasting

Over the course of a lifetime we can strive to develop fluency in many of these spiritual languages. Helping our children become multilingual in the languages of the Spirit by regularly exposing them to many of these languages will expand their spiritual repertoire.

My friend John loves to work in the temple. He particularly delights in wordlessly helping the older people who serve as patrons or workers. Helping others in general is probably John's top signature strength, and serving in the quiet of the temple is one of John's most joyful spiritual languages. He feels at home in the temple and within its walls can hear the voice of the Spirit most clearly. John's wife, Linda, loves talking and counseling with others and sharing their lives with words. Building a home and family is what matters most to Linda. When John and Linda can see the underlying similarities in their spiritual desires despite differences in their native spiritual languages, they more readily support each other despite their differences. They realize that what they are communicating—love for the Lord and a desire to serve His children—is similar even though the language they prefer differs for each of them.

What spiritual languages come most naturally to you? How could you use your top signature strengths in your spiritual life, especially in areas of spirituality you are currently bored with or struggling with?

FROM STRENGTHS TO ABUNDANCE

Christ taught that some influences in this world rob and destroy us but that He came to preserve and nourish us. "I am come that they might have life, and that they might have it more abundantly" (John 10:10).

This doesn't mean we will have an abundance of things or an abundance of accolades or an abundance of advantages. The Savior clarifies later, "And I give unto them eternal life; and they shall never perish, neither shall any man pluck them out of my hand" (John 10:28). The life He came to offer us is eternal life, life with God. We find characteristics of such a life here as we feel our place with the Lord. The abundant life is abundant in beauty, engagement, meaning, and joy.

Abundance implies that we do not just stick with the signature strengths that come most naturally to us but that we also round out our character with strengths of many kinds. Without returning to excessive preoccupation with our weaknesses, we realize that we benefit from flexibility and variety in the strengths on which we rely. We are all capable of most of the signature strengths and spiritual languages to one degree or another. We often come to rely on a few out of habit or familiarity rather than complete incapacity in the others. We can enlarge our sense of abundance by nurturing many virtues and skills, including those that do not come naturally.

In fact, while strengths allow us to go deep into what we do well, weaknesses give us opportunity for innovation and creativity. For example, when we are stuck in an old problem, our best ideas don't always come from our best friends—in fact, they think so much like we do and know us so well that sometimes they have nothing new to say. Weaker relationships with casual acquaintances provide fresher ideas. Likewise, reading in a field we know little about, trying a skill we've never developed, taking a class in an entirely new arena, or trying an interpersonal approach we've never used are ways to practice humility, openness, and living without shame. As we face our fears, we break out of old and vicious cycles and gain confidence in new skills. We get to feel the rapid progress that comes from learning an entirely new skill, rather than always working at familiar skills where improvement comes in much smaller increments. We broaden our exposure to unfamiliar ways of looking at the world that hold high potential for sparking creativity and fresh insight.

God strengthens and empowers us, even when our weaknesses remain. When the word *power* is used in scripture it seems to have two meanings. One is "power over" someone, and this meaning is usually associated with Satan who finds that kind of power enticing. The other meaning is "power to"—power to create, to serve, to live. This is the kind of power God has and desires to share with us. Godly power is grounded in righteous strengths from which to strengthen others.

Even in times of great difficulty or loss, through God's great grace, great strength is born. Living from these strengths helps us find resilience, hope, and meaning. Coupled with faith, humility, and communion with the Spirit of God, such strengths can build Zion, build families, and build sons and daughters of God.

Chapter 8

STRENGTH IN CHRIST

There is nothing that delights me more than to watch my children do what they do well. As I watch one of them extend kindness to others, apply learning to a difficult case, teach with creativity and skill, handle the complexities of relationships, or simply navigate the rigors of adulthood with courage, I feel like I am watching a flower bloom or an eagle soar. My heart swells with quiet joy.

I remember when my first child was born. My mother came to help out for a few days. A day or two after her arrival, she came into my room as I held my little daughter in my arms. Mom seemed eager to say something to me. In fact, I think she had been waiting my whole lifetime to say this. She asked, "Now do you realize just how much I love you?" I think, perhaps for the first time in my life, I did.

I also think, perhaps for the first time in my life, I began to understand something of how much God loves us. He says, "Can a woman forget her suckling child, that she should not have compassion on the son of her womb? yea, they may forget, yet will I not forget thee" (Isaiah 49:15).

It thrills and humbles me to imagine that God takes absolute delight in us as His children and that He desires our happiness at least as much as we desire the happiness of our little ones. The scriptures speak of God's delight and pleasure with those "that deal truly" (Proverbs 12:22) and have faith (see Hebrews 11:6). "The prayer of the upright is his delight" (Proverbs 15:8), as is "the song of the heart" (D&C 25:12). "He delighteth in mercy" (Micah 7:18), in thanksgiving (see Psalm 69:30–31), in obedience (see 1 Samuel 15:22), in "lovingkindness, judgment, and righteousness" (Jeremiah 9:24). These are among the virtues or strengths that when exhibited by His children delight the heart of God.

Of course, He is no stranger to our weaknesses. When Moses complained to God that he was not an orator, God said, "Who hath made man's mouth? or who maketh the dumb, or deaf, or the seeing, or the bind? have not I the Lord? Now therefore go, and I will be with thy mouth, and teach thee what thou shalt say" (Exodus 4:11–12). If we are willing to go when He asks us to go, He will teach us, supplying the gifts we need to complete our mortal assignments. But He is not shocked or dismayed when we need time to learn, to grow from grace to grace.

GRACE TO GRACE

As Christ embarked on His mortal mission, the scriptures record "that he received not of the fulness at the first, but received grace for grace; and . . . continued from grace to grace, until he received a fulness" (D&C 93:12–13). He in turn teaches us, "For if you keep my commandments you shall receive of his fulness, and be glorified in me as I am in the Father; therefore, I say unto you, you shall receive grace for grace" (v. 20).

In the face of my weakness, God offers me grace—strength,

help, tutoring, and power through the mercy and love of the Savior. His Atonement not only redeems me from sin but empowers me in weakness and sanctifies me in strength. It makes me enough to walk back to Him, even in my weakness.

Jesus Christ learned by experience as we must. He did not start out in mortality with a fullness of heavenly power and wisdom but acquired "grace for grace," a little at a time, just as we do. He was devoid of all sin, but He was as subject as I am to the humiliating and limiting—and ultimately empowering and liberating— weakness inherent in being human. He knows how to succor us, empathize with us, and join us.

Christ was a teacher, a healer, an exemplar, a friend, a creator, a peacemaker, a savior. We are deeply comforted and inexorably changed by the compassion and humility Christ acquired through His experience with mortality. We are redeemed and exalted through His saving power and inestimable creative gifts. He came to earth both to suffer for our sins and to lift us with His strength. He invites us to lift one another. Within His embrace our faith matters more than our doubts, our repentance matters more than our sins, our purpose matters more than our fears. Our strength, grounded in Him, matters more than our weakness. These are the promises made possible through His grace.

STRENGTH IN CHRIST

Sometimes God's grace helps us overcome a weakness completely. Sometimes grace empowers us to bless the world, filling us with gratitude for the privilege of being useful in His work. But sometimes our weaknesses just stay weak. When Moroni worries that his weak writing (which remains unchanged) will cause the Gentiles who read it to mock the precious truths he is trying to convey, the Lord simply agrees (see Ether 12:26). God affirms, however, that whether or not the Gentiles have charity is immaterial to Moroni's status with God. God doesn't blame us for how others respond to our weakness, even if it means our weakness seems to undermine His work. What matters is that we are faithful and humble (meek, teachable, and desirous to do God's work, however inadequately). Then we can "be made strong, *even unto the sitting down in the place which I have prepared in the mansions of my Father*" (Ether 12:37; emphasis added). The finest and most important role of grace is not to turn us into Olympic athletes or movie stars. The role of grace is to turn us into friends of God, prepared to sit down with Him in the place He has prepared for us.

The key phrase intervening between our weakness and God's strengthening grace is "if [people] humble themselves before me, and have faith in me" (Ether 12:27). This is a big "if." *If* we allow our weakness to humble us (not shame us or undermine us), then humility will foster virtue; *if* we have faith in Him, then He can work all things together for our good.

I remember a client years ago who absolutely believed in God and absolutely believed in His power and goodness, but she had a difficult illness that had not been cured. She believed she lacked sufficient faith to be healed, and in that belief she had lost all hope of ever meriting a place in God's kingdom. My client did not lack faith—she absolutely believed in God—but she did lack hope, hope that she could gain a place in His kingdom. Hope resides in the understanding that even if we do not "cure" our mortal weaknesses, God wants us to come close. That is how much we matter. That is how valued we are.

The intimacy with which God knows us and desires that we know Him is exactly what Moroni was worried about conveying through his inadequate words. He had read the story of the brother of Jared, who speaks with Jesus face to face, and this story had overpowered him. Moroni was the last faithful person of the entire Jaredite and Nephite civilizations left to fulfill God's promise to the brother of Jared that his story would go to the Gentiles in the last days. And Moroni was left with puny, inadequate words with which to try to convey these amazing realities.

How does one begin to convey, with the best of words, that God is so personal, so humble as to speak with us face to face? How does one tolerate having such an experience trivialized by readers who might not grasp the import of what is being communicated? Even more, how does one tolerate the weakness of being human when confronted with the possibility of coming into the presence of God? This was Moroni's dilemma. How do we look our weakness in the eye and not shrink from the eye of God? Yet this seemingly uncrossable chasm between who we are (weak and fallen) and who God is (perfect and exalted) is spanned completely by the love of God. This is the extent of His reach and His tender care. There are still not words sufficient to portray such love. It can be understood only in the experience of a personal witness.

Moroni is comforted by the promise that if those who read his words will be humble—that all-important qualifier—then their faith will lead to hope, which will lead them to first contemplate and then emulate the charity of God (see Moroni 7:39–45). Charity— the understanding God bestows when we are allowed to grasp how deeply, personally, and passionately God knows and loves each one of us—is the quality that will make us fit for the kingdom of God and prepare us to sit down with Him in the mansions above. When I can receive into my heart how God feels about me, I begin to grasp His goodness. When I can receive into my heart how God feels about you, I begin to grasp charity. How can I belittle, ignore, slight, judge, or mock in any way someone who is so precious? I become long-suffering, patient, gentle, kind, easily entreated. We cannot be jealous or afraid of one another when sharing a place in the arms of such perfect love.

My friend Karen Blake pointed out to me that Ether 12, which actually has the goal and purpose of convincing us that we can know God, pivots around these verses of concern about our human weakness. I had simply never made the connection. I noticed that Moroni was worried about his weakness in writing, even that he compared his writing to that of the brother of Jared, but I had never seen that it was precisely the idea that one can know God in such a personal way that Moroni was both trying to communicate to us and that filled him with trepidation as he faced his weakness. And yet it is this very weakness that God says *He* has given us that—if responded to with humility and when blessed by His grace—can fit us ultimately to sit down with Him as did the brother of Jared.

Moroni leaves us with his witness, which is in essence, God told me that even though fools mock, even though we feel so inadequate and weak, human weakness is designed to draw us close to God, not separate us from Him (see Ether 12:26–28). If we will allow weakness to make us humble and honest, these qualities in turn can make us hopeful and charitable, and this will fit us to know God because we will be more like Him. We become capable of seeing Him when our lives reflect the charity and humility He embodies.

Our weakness is not just in our skill deficits and human frailties. Our weakness is not just in our lack of writing skill to express our experience with God. Our weakness is in our very capacity to hold that experience, to tolerate such love. We are too weak to hold intimacy with God for more than glimpses and moments of earthly time. His goodness and mercy are so personal they overpower not only the capacity of our words but the capacity of our hearts.

SEEING MY WEAKNESS

Over a period of several days I recently prayed about my sins and weaknesses. As I read the scriptures I tried to pay particular attention to commandments I might be ignoring. I asked God to help me have eyes to see, that my weaknesses might become more apparent. I expected that God would have a long list to show me of the ways I am not sufficiently charitable, obedient, or self-sacrificing.

After a few days a quotation from President Brigham Young, part of a longer personal account, was sent to me by a friend. It reads: "You that have not passed thro' the trials and persecutions, and drivings with this people from the beginning, but have only read them, or heard some of them related, may think how awful they were to endure, and wonder that the saints survived them at all.— The thought of it makes your heart sink within you, your brain reel, and your body tremble, and you are ready to exclaim, 'I could not have endured it.' I have been in the heat of it, and never felt better in all my life; I never felt the peace and power of the Almighty more copiously poured upon me than in the keenest part of our trials. They appeared nothing to me."[1]

With you, I worry about the state of the world, my country, and my own household as I try to prepare for various eventualities. Sometimes instead of becoming prepared I simply become afraid— afraid of what might happen, afraid of how I will cope. Brigham Young is right: I often wonder how the Saints endured, and the thought of what might yet lie ahead for us makes my heart sink and my brain reel and my body tremble. I am sure I could not survive, and what is more, I want to be sure God knows I could not survive. That fear is not constructive, but it has seemed to me inevitable. Sometimes the fear prompts me to action, but mostly it prompts me to whine. It seems some part of me is afraid not to be afraid—afraid if I admit God's comforting presence is sufficient then He will expect me to be brave instead of protecting me from threat.

Brigham Young's experience opened up another door, and as I looked through it I saw a world where serenity and peace exist in the midst of turmoil, even more than in their absence. I realized that my weakness was not in my unwillingness to make sufficient sacrifices, which is what I expected the Spirit to whisper. My weakness, the one God wanted me to humbly bring to Him, was my unwillingness to receive God's grace as enough. Even if God does not spare us hardship, He can spare us despair. The comfort and sustenance of the Spirit can truly be enough if we will let them in. My problem is less my struggle to sacrifice and obey and more my struggle to receive. This is not just true as I anticipate the signs of the times. This is true in my home, with my loved ones, and in my daily work. God's grace is sufficient to fill my heart with joy and peace today, even if my life is marred by hidden wounds, even if my children's hopes are not all realized, even if loss invades.

President John Taylor writes: "I know that as other men we have our trials, afflictions, sorrows, and privations. We meet with difficulties; we have to contend with the world, with the powers of darkness, with the corruptions of men, and a variety of evils; yet at the same time through these things we have to be made perfect. It is necessary that we should have a knowledge of ourselves, of our true position and standing before God, and comprehend our strength and weakness; our ignorance and intelligence; our wisdom and our folly, that we may know how to appreciate true principles, and comprehend and put a proper value upon all things as they present themselves before our minds.

"It is necessary that we should know our own weaknesses, and the weaknesses of our fellow men; our own strength as well as the strength of others; and comprehend our true position before God, angels, and men; that we may be inclined to treat all with due respect, and not to over value our own wisdom or strength, nor deprecate it, nor that of others; but put our trust in the living God, and follow after him, and realise that we are his children, and that he is our Father, and that our dependence is upon him, and that every blessing we receive flows from his beneficent hand."[2]

STRENGTHS WE DO NOT SEE

I began this book with a story about my mission where I learned that God called me to contribute from my strengths, not to fret over my weaknesses. I would like to end this book with another mission story, not my own, but one that seems to suggest a different conclusion.

My friend Elizabeth and her husband, Howard, felt strongly that when their last child left for his mission, they should do the same. They sold their home, put their affairs in order, and put in their papers. Elizabeth is one of my favorite Relief Society teachers, and I couldn't help but think of all the places in the Church where young adults in particular would benefit from her skill. I encouraged her to apply for a position in the Church Educational System, where her considerable teaching strength could bless the youth of the Church. But Elizabeth and her husband felt they should submit their papers and accept whatever calling was extended.

Their call came for Moscow, Russia. This may not be the most difficult mission in the world, but it is not the easiest. Elizabeth and Howard would have a difficult language to learn, a new culture to assimilate, and few familiar comforts. Elizabeth's hardest challenge came as they were to board the plane for the final leg of their journey to Moscow. A darkness and fear came over her that almost stopped her in her tracks. But she got on the plane.

Howard and Elizabeth recently returned from their mission and gave a report in our ward. Elizabeth said, in essence, "The Lord did not call me to Russia for my strengths. Instead the Lord probed my weaknesses. I love reading and learning about all aspects of the gospel, but for eighteen months the only thing I had to read was the standard works. I struggled terrifically with the Russian language. I could not understand or participate in the church meetings where the gospel was taught. I could not participate in a gospel discussion with any of the local people. I could not teach the things I loved. I felt lucky if I could discern what the general topic of a conversation or a class was, but I got none of the details.

"In addition, I am a terrible cook who can't make a thing without a recipe and can't remember the recipe even if it is for something I've made a hundred times. But recipes were useless in a country where the food is so different and familiar items are unavailable. Yet I was cooking for the missionaries constantly with whatever we could find.

"Most of what we did consisted of traveling by bus in horrible heat or freezing cold from one place to another to support a branch, meet with an inactive member, help the missionaries, teach a class; then getting up the next day and doing it again, and again. Each day we tried to do these simple tasks a little better than the day before. There were no great spiritual victories, just trying to support others as best we could in living the gospel day by day.

"But this is what I learned from the Russian people: to endure. When Communism fell and the economy collapsed, there was almost no food available in the stores and no money to buy it with. They raised little gardens. They stood in lines for hours every day. They endured. They have this incredible patience. They don't give up. They made do, and they got by with nothing. They get up every day and try to do a little better at the same familiar tasks. And they are incredibly strong."

I knew as Elizabeth spoke of the tenacity, patience, and endurance of the Russian people in times of great hardship that we may face similar times in this country and in our personal lives. As we do, Elizabeth's experience will bless my life and the lives of all she shares it with. I can't help but think that it is not just the preparation we have made with food storage and 72-hour kits that will save us in such times. It is the preparation of people like Elizabeth who have not only developed deep reserves but have given us a vision of what it means to be patient, to be resilient, to be strong. In such circumstances perhaps we will be sustained by hope even if we have little bread—by images and stories of endurance and patience, opening our hearts to the Spirit's willing gifts of peace, hope, even joy.

Elizabeth saw her mission as a probing of her weakness because the strengths with which she most identifies were not called on. But Elizabeth emerged from her mission with new strengths, not core to her extant identity but core to her truest self: resilience, patience, charity, persistence, and making do. She and Howard hope to return for another mission to Russia at some future date. Perhaps I too will one day long to return to the places where I learned by hard experience the most important lessons of life.

One of the senior missionaries in our mission shared with us this counsel: "In all times and in all places, teach of Christ. If necessary, use words."

Elizabeth, and through her words the Russian people, taught me about the amazing strengths that come through weakness. The sermon she spoke and the one she lived remind me of the words of Ammon: "I know that I am nothing; as to my strength I am weak;

therefore I will not boast of myself, but I will boast of my God, for in his strength I can do all things" (Alma 26:12).

Moroni concludes his chapter on weakness and strength with these words: "I have seen Jesus, and . . . he hath talked with me face to face, and . . . told me in plain humility, even as a man telleth another in mine own language, concerning these things; and only a few have I written, because of my weakness in writing. And now, I would commend you to seek this Jesus of whom the prophets and apostles have written, that the grace of God the Father, and also the Lord Jesus Christ, and the Holy Ghost, which beareth record of them, may be and abide in you forever. Amen" (Ether 12:39–41).

Moroni completes his compelling testimony with these verses near the very end of the Book of Mormon: "Yea, come unto Christ, and be perfected in him, and deny yourselves of all ungodliness; and if ye shall deny yourselves of all ungodliness, and love God with all your might, mind and strength, then is his grace sufficient for you, that by his grace ye may be perfect in Christ; and if by the grace of God ye are perfect in Christ, ye can in nowise deny the power of God. And again, if ye by the grace of God are perfect in Christ, and deny not his power, then are ye sanctified in Christ by the grace of God, through the shedding of the blood of Christ, which is in the covenant of the Father unto the remission of your sins, that ye become holy, without spot" (Moroni 10:32–33).

By right of our covenant relationship with God, our willing obedience, and our humble petitions, we are entitled to this grace, this enabling power of God as our Father, Jesus as our Redeemer, and the Holy Ghost as our Comforter. Their grace is sufficient to compensate for every human sin and weakness, to make us holy and without spot, and this, in the humble words of Nephi, "notwithstanding [our] weakness" (2 Nephi 33:11).

---⟡---

ACKNOWLEDGMENTS

I t is not lost on me that Moroni's lament about his weakness is set off by his efforts to write about the things of God, especially as he compared his work to the powerful words of more capable others (Ether 12:19–25). There is so much room to be misunderstood when trying to describe sacred things that can be taught adequately only by the Holy Ghost, and yet there is nothing more crucial to *not* have misunderstood. Moroni undertook this task alone, without earthly editors, friends, or colleagues to assist him.

Blessedly, the rest of us have access to human support in such humbling endeavors. I am blessed by wonderful friends ho shape not only my thinking but my soul: Karen Blake, Kathleen· Flake, Christine Packard, Richard Ferre, and especially my family—Dave, Carrie, Monika, Mike, and Melanie. It is no longer possible for me to delineate where their ideas end off and mine begin, so I apologize to t hem all in advance for my relentless plagiarism.

This list could quickly get too long to contain, but must also include John, Linda Beth, Moni, Nancy, Wayne, Thom, Helen, and Lynn, among many others. I am grateful for professional mentors—

Allen Bergin, Scott Richards, David Klimek, and colleagues at the Association of Mormon Counselors and Psychotherapists, who have believed in me and nurtured me along.

I am eternally thankful for wonderful brothers and sisters in wards in Santa Monica, Ann Arbor, and Alpine, and for the members and missionaries of the Canada Montreal Mission. In these places and with these Saints I have feasted at banquets of charity and tasted Zion.

I deeply appreciate the staff at Deseret Book for their skillful guidance and plain hard work, including Cory Maxwell for countless e-mails more carefully crafted than my best prose, Laurel Christensen for the initial concept for this book, Suzanne Brady for thoughtful editing, Shauna Gibby for the cover design, and Rachael Ward for the typography. I am so grateful to Michelle Holt, Judy Seegmiller, Myriam and her staff, the team at Time Out for Women, and Kathy, Rita, Marilyn, and Tara for their professional skills and great kindness.

I thank Dave Ulrich, Ralph Christensen, Christine Packard, Nancy Brockbank, Marleen Williams, Karen Blake, Brent Top, and Virginia Pearce for thoughtful feedback on early drafts of this book. I humbly acknowledge the clients who have shared their journeys and life lessons with me.

I honor and thank my parents, Les and Barbara Woolsey; my in-laws Karin and Richard Ulrich and Belinda Woodson and her great kids; my brother, Eric Woolsey, and my sweet sister, Carla Hickman, and their beautiful families; and my extended family, especially my sweet aunts and inspiring grandmothers.

But of course my deepest gratitude is due to Those I do not now see whose influence on my life is beyond the capacity of my weak words to describe—bringing me back to where I began, in the good company of Moroni, whose concern about his weakness prompted a Divine response (Ether 12:27) that provides the foundational concept for this book.

NOTES

CHAPTER 2: DISTINGUISHING SIN FROM WEAKNESS

1. Orson F. Whitney, *Saturday Night Thoughts* (Salt Lake City, 1927), 241–42. Quoted in *Encyclopedia of Mormonism*, ed. Daniel Ludlow (New York: Macmillan, 1992), 1314.

2. LDS Bible Dictionary, s.v. "Repentance," 760–61.

3. Boyd K. Packer, "The Brilliant Morning of Forgiveness," *Ensign*, November 1995, 19–20.

4. LDS Bible Dictionary, s.v. "Grace," 697.

5. See David H. Stern, *Complete Jewish Bible* (Clarksville, Md.: Jewish New Testament Publications, 1998).

CHAPTER 3: INCREASING SELF-AWARENESS, AVOIDING SELF-DECEPTION

1. Spencer W. Kimball, "'Give Me This Mountain,'" *Ensign*, November 1979, 78.

2. I am grateful to Karen Blake (personal conversation) for her insight into this parable.

3. LDS Bible Dictionary, s.v. "Repentance," 760–61.

CHAPTER 4: HUMILITY: THE "REPENTANCE" FOR WEAKNESS

1. Ezra Taft Benson, "Beware of Pride," *Ensign*, May 1989, 4–6.

2. F. Enzio Busche, "Love Is the Power That Will Cure the Family," *Ensign*, May 1982, 70.

3. Daniel Goleman, *Social Intelligence: The Revolutionary New Science of Human Relationships* (New York: Bantam Dell, 2006), 82.

4. F. Enzio Busche, "Truth Is the Issue," *Ensign*, November 1993, 24.

5. Terrence C. Smith, "An Anatomy of Troubles," AMCAP Convention, October 3, 2008, 8.

6. Neal A. Maxwell, *Notwithstanding My Weakness* (Salt Lake City: Deseret Book, 1981), 5.

7. Ibid., 3.

8. High Nibley, *Of All Things*, ed. Gary P. Gillum (Salt Lake City: Signature Books, 1981), 5, as quoted in Tad R. Callister, *The Infinite Atonement* (Salt Lake City: Deseret Book, 2000), 275.

CHAPTER 5: OVERCOMING SHAME, STRENGTHENING HUMILITY

1. Neal A. Maxwell, *Notwithstanding My Weakness* (Salt Lake City: Deseret Book, 1981), 9.

2. Lane Fischer, "The Shame Matrix: Shame, Grief, and Hope in Psychotherapy," plenary address at the Association of Mormon Counselors and Psychotherapists Convention, October 2008.

3. Ibid.

4. Beverly Flanigan, *Forgiving the Unforgivable* (New York: Collier Books, 1994), 93.

CHAPTER 6: WHEN I AM WEAK, THEN AM I STRONG

1. LDS Bible Dictionary, s.v. "Grace," 697.

2. Jacques Lusseyran, *And There Was Light: Autobiography of Jacques Lusseyran, Blind Hero of the French Resistance*, trans. Elizabeth R. Cameron, 2d ed. (New York: Parabola Books, 1998), 16–17.

3. Ibid., 19–21.

4. Neal A. Maxwell, *Notwithstanding My Weakness* (Salt Lake City: Deseret Book, 1981), 9, 10.

CHAPTER 7: LIVING FROM STRENGTHS

1. Sonja Lyubomirsky, *The How of Happiness: A Scientific Approach to Getting the Life You Want* (New York: Penguin Press, 2007), 39.

2. Martin E. P. Seligman, *Authentic Happiness: Using the New Positive Psychology to Realize Your Potential for Lasting Fulfillment* (New York: Free Press, 2002), 248–49.

3. Martin E. P. Seligman, Tracy A. Steen, Nansook Park, and Christopher Peterson, "Positive Psychology Progress: Empirical Validation of Interventions," in *American Psychologist* 60, no. 5 (July–August, 2005): 412.

4. Ibid., 419–20.

5. Ibid., 420.

6. David Milne, "People Can Learn Markers on the Road to Resilience," *Psychiatric News* 42, no. 2 (January 19, 2007): 5.

CHAPTER 8: STRENGTH IN CHRIST

1. *Deseret News Weekly*, 24 Aug. 1854, 83, quoted by L. Aldin Porter, "'But We Heeded Them Not,'" *Ensign*, August 1998, 6.

2. *John Taylor*, in Teachings of Presidents of the Church series (Salt Lake City: The Church of Jesus Christ of Latter-day Saints, 2001): 203.

INDEX

ABOUT THE AUTHOR

Wendy Ulrich, Ph.D., is a fellow and former president of the Association of Mormon Counselors and Psychotherapists and has been a psychologist in private practice in Michigan for over twenty years. She is founder of Sixteen Stones Center for Growth in Utah, offering seminar-retreats on forgiveness, abundance, loss, and spirituality. A former ward and stake Relief Society president, she recently served with her husband in presiding over the Canada Montreal Mission. They have three children.